MANTRAS FOR THE MIDNIGHT

ROBERT F. MORNEAU

Mantras for the
MIDNIGHT

Reflections for the Night Country

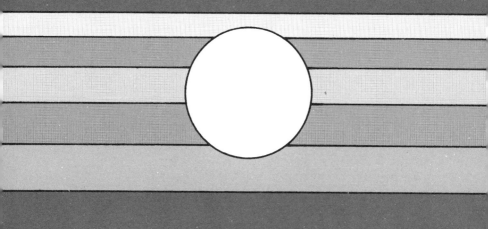

THE LITURGICAL PRESS
Collegeville, Minnesota

2   3   4   5   6   7   8

Cover design by Cathleen Casey.

ISBN 0-8146-1404-3

Library of Congress Cataloging in Publication Data

Morneau, Robert F., 1938–
    Mantras for the midnight.
    1. Meditations. 2. Prayers. I. Title.
BX2182.2.M6675   1985   242   85-24231
ISBN 0-8146-1404-3

*Midnight is not the time
to greet a guest . . .*

CONTENTS

8   *Contents*

THE HOUSE AT REST
by Jessica Powers

On a dark night
Kindled in love with yearnings—
Oh, happy chance!—
I went forth unobserved,
My house being now at rest.
                    —St. John of the Cross

How does one hush one's house,
each proud possessive wall, each sighing rafter,
the rooms made restless with remembered laughter
or wounding echoes, the permissive doors,
the stairs that vacillate from up to down,
windows that bring in color and event
from countryside or town,
oppressive ceilings and complaining floors?

The house must first of all accept the night.
Let it erase the walls and their display,
impoverish the rooms till they are filled
with humble silences; let clocks be stilled
and all the selfish urgencies of the day.

Midnight is not the time to greet a guest.
Caution the doors against both foes and friends,
and try to make the windows understand
their unimportance when the daylight ends.
Persuade the stairs to patience, and deny
the passages their aimless to and fro.
Virtue it is that puts a house at rest.
How well repaid that tenant is, how blest
who, when the call is heard,
is free to take his kindled heart and go.[1]

ACKNOWLEDGEMENTS

The author acknowledges the generous and expert assistance of these people who contributed their time and talent to make this book possible:

For their photography on the pages indicated:

JULIE BRUSKY: 79, 120, 127, 134; NICKI DAVIS: 58, 97, 122, 126; REV. ROBERT K. FINNEGAN, O. PRAEM.: 74, 110, 145; ANN HOLLENBACK: 53, 107; REV. ROBERT LALIBERTE: 32, 34, 39, 48, 117, 132, 140; REV. AARON J. WALSCHINSKI, O. PRAEM.: 19, 42, 71, 76, 91, 112; KIT WOESSNER: 37, 50, 86, 89; other photos by the author.

SISTER MIRIAM CECILE ROSS, S.S.N.D., for the music; SISTER MARY DE SALES HOFFMANN, O.S.F., and SISTER MARIE ISABEL MCELRONE, O.S.F., for editorial assistance;

ROSEMARY BOMBERG and KATE NEUMANN for their typing.

DOUBLEDAY AND CO., INC.: *Anne Frank: The Diary of a Young Girl,* translated from the Dutch by B. M. Mooyaart-Doubleday. Copyright © 1952 by Otto H. Frank; Goethe's *Faust,* translated by Walter Kaufmann. Copyright © 1961 by Walter Kaufmann; *The Cloud of Unknowing and the Book of Privy Counseling,* newly edited with an introduction by William Johnston. Copyright © 1973 by William Johnston. Selections reprinted by permission of Image Books, a Division of Doubleday and Co., Inc.

FARRAR, STRAUS AND GIROUX, INC.: *The Habit of Being* by Flannery O'Connor, letters with an introduction by Sally Fitzgerald. Copyright © 1979 by Regina O'Connor; *Wandering: Notes and Sketches* by Hermann Hesse, translated by James Wright. Translation Copyright © 1972 by Farrar, Straus and Giroux, Inc.

GROVE PRESS: Poem "#91," by e. e. cummings, from the book *100 Selected Poems.* Copyright © 1926 by Horace Liveright; 1923, 1925, 1931, 1935, 1938, 1939, 1940, 1944, 1945, 1947, 1948, 1949, 1950 by e. e. cummings.

HARCOURT BRACE JOVANOVICH, INC.: *The Unexpected Universe* by Loren Eiseley. Copyright © 1969 by Loren Eiseley.

HARPER & ROW, INC.: *Meister Eckhart,* translated by Raymond Blakney. Copyright © 1941 by Harper & Row, Inc.

HOLT, RINEHART AND WINSTON, INC.: Poem "Acquainted with the Night" by Robert Frost, from the book, *The Poetry of Robert Frost,* edited by Edward Connery Lathem. Copyright © 1928, 1969 by Holt, Rinehart and Winston. Copyright © 1956 by Robert Frost. Reprinted by permission of Holt, Rinehart and Winston, Publishers.

INSTITUTE FOR CARMELITE STUDIES (ICS PUBLICATIONS): *The Complete Works of St. John of the Cross,* translated by Kieran Kavanaugh, O.C.D., and Otilio Rodriguez, O.C.D. Copyright © 1973 by the Washington Province of Discalced Carmelites, Inc.; *Story of a Soul: The Autobiography of St. Thérèse of Lisieux* translated by John Clarke, O.C.D. Copyright © 1975 by the Washington Province of Discalced Carmelites.

ALFRED A. KNOPF, INC.: *Markings* by Dag Hammarskjold, translated by Leif Sjoberg and W. H. Auden. Copyright © 1964 by Alfred A. Knopf, Inc. and Faber and Faber, Ltd.; *A Flag for Sunrise* by Robert Stone. Copyright © 1977, 1980, 1981 by Robert Stone.

MACMILLAN, INC.: *The Denial of Death* by Ernest Becker. Copyright © 1973 by the Free Press, a Division of Macmillan, Inc.

NEW DIRECTIONS PUBLISHING CORP.: *Seeds of Contemplation* by Thomas Merton. Copyright © 1949 by Our Lady of Gethsemani Monastery.

HAROLD OBER ASSOCIATES, INC.: *Newman: The Pillar of the Cloud* by Meriol Trevor. Copyright © 1962 by Meriol Trevor.

PAULIST PRESS: From the series Classics of Western Spirituality: *Purgation and Purgatory: The Spiritual Dialogue* by Catherine of Genoa, translated by Serge Hughes. Copyright © 1979; *The Dialogue* by Catherine of Siena, translated by Suzanne Noffke, O.P. Copyright © 1980; *Showings: Julian of Norwich,* translated by Edmund Colledge, O.S.A., and James Walsh, S.J. Copyright © 1978; *The Interior Castle* by Teresa of Avila, translated by Kieran Kavanaugh, O.C.D., and Otilio Rodriguez, O.C.D. Copyright © 1979. The above works, with the exception of *The Interior Castle* by Teresa of Avila, which copyright is owned by the Washington Province of Discalced Carmelites, Inc., are copyrighted by The Missionary Society of St. Paul the Apostle in the State of New York.

JESSICA POWERS: *The House at Rest.* Copyright © 1984 by Jessica Powers.

RANDOM HOUSE, INC.: *The Divine Comedy* by Dante Alighieri, translated by Lawrence Grant White. Copyright © 1948 by Pantheon Books, Inc., a Division of Random House, Inc.; *Memories, Dreams and Reflections* by C. G. Jung, translated by Richard and Clara Winston, edited by Aniela Jaffe. Translation Copyright © 1961, 1962, 1963 by Random House, Inc. Reprinted with permission from Pantheon Books, Inc., a Division of Random House, Inc.; *The Confessions of Nat Turner* by William Styron. Copyright © 1966, 1967 by William Styron.

SIMON AND SCHUSTER, INC. *Ways of Escape* by Graham Greene. Copyright © 1980 by Graham Greene.

REGNERY GATEWAY, INC.: *The Lord* by Romano Guardini, translated by Elinor Castendyk Briefs. Copyright © 1954 by the Henry Regnery Co.

PREFACE

The prophet Isaiah writes:

> *The people who walked in darkness*
> *have seen a great light;*
> *Upon those who dwelt in the land of gloom*
> *a light has shone.* (Isaiah 9:1)

The land of darkness and gloom is a frequented spot for many of us. Though we desire light and joy, many of our human experiences actually veil the light and move us toward despair. War, rejection, abandonment, failure, sin, fear—this is the night country. We tend to deny and thus repress these elements of life; the challenge is to look them in the face and assume our proper responsibility. Only then will light dispel the darkness; only then will gloom give way to hope.

This volume of mantras is for the "midnight"—that mysterious and lonely time between dusk and dawn. It is a unique place and a unique time, traveled and experienced by and large alone. Few forms of escape are available: daytime noise, hurried calendars, urgent appointments, busy leisure. Nothing remains here but the dark and the silence calling us to meet Reality. At this trysting place even a whispered mantra is an intrusion into our innermost sanctuary and must be discarded when the Light comes. For it is in the dark that the Lord comes to bless and confront his people and we await his visitation in fear and trembling.

Previous volumes, *Mantras for the Morning* and *Mantras for the Evening*, focus on themes more buoyant than those contained in this book. There is a reason for that. A friend accosted me with the accusation that the previous reflections failed to penetrate deeply enough into the paschal mystery, into the cross and dark side of our journey. Though unsaid, the implication was that the earlier volumes were somewhat romantic, almost too positive. The element of truth in the accusation has led to this journey into the midnight. For some the experiences shared may be too dark; for others, not dark enough. There are shades of darkness at midnight as there are varying degrees of light at noon. Much depends upon where we are standing and who we are. We place our hope in the Lord knowing that with the dawn there will be rejoicing.

I.
Midnight Mantras
and the Word of God

Lostness

MANTRA: **Master, Master, we are lost!**

SOURCE: Luke 8:22-25

One day he got into a boat with his disciples and said to them, "Let us cross over to the far side of the lake." So they set out, and as they sailed he slept. A windstorm descended on the lake, and they began to ship water and to be in danger. They came to awaken him, saying, "Master, master, we are lost!" He awoke and rebuked the wind and the tumultuous waves. The waves subsided and it grew calm. Then he asked them, "Where is your faith?" Filled with fear and admiration, they said to one another, "What sort of man can this be who commands even the winds and the sea and they obey him?"

PARALLEL REFERENCES

The breakers of death surged round about me,
   the destroying floods overwhelmed me;
The cords of the nether world enmeshed me,
   the snares of death overtook me.
In my distress I called upon the LORD
   and cried out to my God;
From his temple he heard my voice,
   and my cry to him reached his ears. *(Psalm 18:5-7)*

My soul is deprived of peace,
   I have forgotten what happiness is;
I tell myself my future is lost,
   all that I hoped for from the LORD.

18

The thought of my homeless poverty
  is wormwood and gall;
Remembering it over and over
  leaves my soul downcast within me.
But I will call this to mind,
   as my reason to have hope. *(Lamentations 3:17-21)*

Mas - ter, Mas - ter, we are lost!

LOST AND FOUND

MASTER, MASTER, WE ARE LOST!
MASTER, MASTER, WE ARE LOST!

> Small global village in a vast universe . . . hurrying
> and scurrying around a small and insignificant star . . .
> generations come and go like autumn leaves—Lord, give
> us faith to see.

MASTER, MASTER, WE ARE LOST!
MASTER, MASTER, WE ARE LOST!

> Our individual planets collide in pain . . . trying to
> understand in vast darkness . . . trying to love though
> yards apart . . . lost in petty fears, hardened hearts—
> Lord, teach us to love.

MASTER, MASTER, WE ARE LOST!
MASTER, MASTER, WE ARE LOST!

> Pounding waves erode our soft foundations . . . ungentle
> seas draw us into chaos . . . twisting, turning rapids
> break bones and crush skulls . . . flooding rivers erase
> all markings—Lord, still the waters of our panic and pain.

MASTER, MASTER, WE ARE LOST!
MASTER, MASTER, WE ARE LOST!

> Compass lost . . . oars abandoned . . . sails torn and
> tattered . . . rudder rock-destroyed . . . hull twisted
> and broken—Lord, captain our hearts and lives.

Mas - ter, Mas - ter, we are lost!

PRAYER

Lord Jesus, our journey is filled with many unknowns. So easily we lose our sense of direction and fail to follow in your way. Reveal once again the map that leads to you; show us the path we are to walk; guide us according to your will. *Amen.*

QUOTATIONS FROM GRAHAM GREENE

A friendship can be a way of escape, just as much as writing or travel, from the everyday routine, the sense of failure, the fear of the future.

———

We have lost the power of clear action because we have lost the ability to believe.

———

The vision of faith as an untroubled sea was lost forever; faith was more like a tempest in which the lucky were engulfed and lost, and the unfortunate survived to be flung battered and bleeding on the shore.

———

Peace he was not granted — only a long despair which he passed off with the lighter word, boredom.

———

Writing is a form of therapy; sometimes I wonder how all those who do not write, compose or paint can manage to escape the madness, the melancholia, the panic fear which is inherent in the human situation.[2]

LOSTNESS

The train whistle knifes its way through the dark night, its haunting sound finding lodging in the human soul. How else explain its enigmatic affinity with that melancholic sound?

Behind the appealing façade of apparent orientation and happy serenity, each of us knows in more honest moments that our journey through time and space is radically grounded in faith. Our own planet earth, hurling through an incomprehensibly vast universe, seems lost in space. Wrapped up in our daily tasks and simple loves, we so easily disregard our feeling of lostness and the perplexing questions it invites. But the night train interrupts our restless sleep and forces our soul to ponder.

Judas tasted lostness and found a tree; Peter's words created a void which he allowed tears and forgiveness to fill. Thomas touched the gouged-out wounds and believed; John entered the empty tomb and found the Risen Lord. Job was stripped of all he loved and learned to trust; David lost the son of his sin and found the Lord's love once again.

In desperation we study maps and books to chart our place in the sun. Yet the night whistle causes the soul to tremble as the rumbling tracks shake our books on their shelves. We sit naked and alone seeking to be found as we seek to find.

Our God has come to live in this lostness—he walks our endless roads, he gazes into the darkness of the starry night, he shares our broken relationships and lost loves. His presence redeems the lostness. It is gathered up into the arms of love and carried back home. He has tasted the lostness from the inside. The train whistle's mournful echo has given birth to peace and joy in the human soul.

Betrayal

MANTRA: **The hand of my betrayer**

SOURCE: Luke 22:21-23

". . . And yet the hand of my betrayer is with me at this table. The Son of Man is following out his appointed course, but woe to that man by whom he is betrayed." Then they began to dispute among themselves as to which of them would do such a deed.

PARALLEL REFERENCES

"You stiff-necked people, uncircumcised in heart and ears, you are always opposing the Holy Spirit just as your fathers did before you. Was there ever any prophet whom your fathers did not persecute? In their day, they put to death those who foretold the coming of the Just One; now you in your turn have become his betrayers and murderers. You who received the law through the ministry of angels have not observed it."   *(Acts 7:51-53)*

The next morning David wrote a letter to Joab which he sent by Uriah. In it he directed: "Place Uriah up front, where the fighting is fierce. Then pull back and leave him to be struck down dead." So while Joab was besieging the city, he assigned Uriah to a place where he knew the defenders were strong. When the men of the city made a sortie against Joab, some officers of David's army fell, and among them Uriah the Hittite died.   *(2 Samuel 11:14-17)*

SILVER PIECES — THIRTY!

THE HAND OF MY BETRAYER,
THE HAND OF MY BETRAYER,

BETRAYAL

stones thrown at the window of one's heart
a hug turned into a strangle-hold
a glass of wine tainted with poison
a walk through an autumn woods to an ambush
the scattering of weeds in the field of love
the planting of suspicion in the heart of a friend
the arms of hospitality violated by lust

THE HAND OF MY BETRAYER,
THE HAND OF MY BETRAYER,

HAND

extended in peace — to deliver a blow
opened in friendship — to be fisted in hate
created for love — to be destroyed by selfishness
the hand of a friend — surrendered for thirty pieces of silver

THE HAND OF MY BETRAYER,
THE HAND OF MY BETRAYER.

The hand of my be - tray - er

PRAYER

Lord God, our hands are not pure. Stained by greed and indifference, scarred by suspicion and fear, we need your surgeon's knife to mend our nerves and heal our broken bones. Forgive us our betrayals, large and small; make us whole again. Restore our hands to fidelity and love. We ask this in Jesus, the man betrayed. *Amen.*

QUOTATIONS FROM C. S. LEWIS

There are only two kinds of people in the end: those who say to God, "Thy will be done," and those to whom God says, in the end, "*Thy* will be done."

". . . every poet and musician and artist, but for Grace, is drawn away from love of the thing he tells, to love of the telling till, down in Deep Hell, they cannot be interested in God at all but only in what they say about Him. For it doesn't stop at being interested in paint, you know. They sink lower—become interested in their own personalities and then in nothing but their own reputations."

"Pam, Pam—no natural feelings are high or low, holy or unholy, in themselves. They are all holy when God's hand is on the rein. They all go bad when they set up on their own and make themselves into false gods."

There is but one good: that is God. Everything else is good when it looks to Him and bad when it turns from Him.[3]

THE COCK'S CROW

I heard it twice—once in Nazareth, a second time in Assisi. Both times it was early dawn; both times it woke me from a restless sleep. It was the cock's crow.

Jesus' prediction involving Peter echoes throughout history. The ability to disassociate oneself from friendship and to turn one's loved ones over to an enemy germinates within every human heart. The compulsion for survival, the fear of suffering, the yielding to intimidation—all these forms of egoism lead us into infidelity and loss of integrity.

The cock's crowing is meant to welcome the dawn and newness of life. It need not awaken us to despair. Grace and discipline are needed lest we yield to that radical self-preservation that excludes faithfulness. Alone, our weakness is overwhelming; graced, we are empowered to sacrifice what is dearest and nearest. The morning call of the cock is an invitation to pray for the grace of fidelity. Relationships vary in intensity. Though betrayal focuses on those major friendships we have, we must recognize that "small" betrayals can exist at every level: a promise made and not kept, a responsibility accepted and then ignored, a commitment professed only to be discarded, a hope held out and then smashed without care. Fidelity in large matters is contingent on these smaller daily acts of faithfulness.

Lord, forgive us for betraying you and one another in allowing conversations to continue that injure another's reputation, in creating expectations in others that we never intend to fulfill, in refusing to sit in your presence in silence and solitude, in remaining quiet when lies are told, in neglecting to say the soft word while another is in pain. Lord, heal our sickness — may the cock's crowing tell only of a faithful Son.

Unbelief

MANTRA: **I will never believe it**

SOURCE: John 20:24-29

It happened that one of the Twelve, Thomas (the name means "Twin"), was absent when Jesus came. The other disciples kept telling him: "We have seen the Lord!" His answer was, "I will never believe it without probing the nail-prints in his hands, without putting my finger in the nail-marks and my hand into his side."

A week later, the disciples were once more in the room, and this time Thomas was with them. Despite the locked doors, Jesus came and stood before them. "Peace be with you," he said; then, to Thomas: "Take your finger and examine my hands. Put your hand into my side. Do not persist in your unbelief, but believe!" Thomas said in response, "My Lord and my God!" Jesus said to him:
"You became a believer because you saw me.
Blest are they who have not seen and have believed."

PARALLEL REFERENCES

Faith is confident assurance concerning what we hope for, and conviction about things we do not see. Because of faith the men of old were approved by God. Through faith we perceive that the worlds were created by the word of God, and that what is visible came into being through the invisible. By faith Abel offered God a sacrifice greater than Cain's. Because of this he was attested to be just, God himself having borne witness to him on account of his gifts; therefore, although Abel is dead, he still speaks. By faith Enoch was taken away without dying, and "he was seen no more because God took him." Scripture testifies that, before he was taken up, he was pleasing to God—but without faith, it is impossible to please him. Anyone who comes to God must believe that he exists, and that he rewards those who seek him. *(Hebrews 11:1-6)*

From this time on, many of his disciples broke away and would not remain in his company any longer. Jesus then said to the Twelve, "Do you want to leave me too?" Simon Peter answered him, "Lord, to whom shall we go? You have the words of eternal life. We have come to believe; we are convinced that you are God's holy one."
(John 6:66-69)

WITHOUT SEEING

I WILL NEVER BELIEVE IT,
I WILL NEVER BELIEVE IT—

> I will never believe that
> > a caterpillar can fly
> > an acorn can become an oak tree
> > an enemy can become a friend
> > in silence there is sound
> > death opens to life
> > the deaf will hear
> > the blind will see
> > tombs will one day be empty

I WILL NEVER BELIEVE IT,
I WILL NEVER BELIEVE IT—

> And yet
> > butterflies fill the August sky
> > oak trees give birth to millions of acorns
> > sounds of silence provide gentle hymns
> > stones are rolled back and wrappings lie neatly folded
> > the sightless see and the deaf hear
> > the cross makes enemies friends

I WILL NEVER BELIEVE IT,
I WILL NEVER BELIEVE IT—BUT I DO.

I will nev-er be-lieve it

PRAYER

Risen and living Lord, it is the nail-prints that lead us to faith. Through your love and obedience on the cross, you reveal the extravagant concern of your Father. Fill us with the spirit of faith that we may truly believe that you dwell within our hearts. Fill us with Easter joy and hope. *Amen.*

QUOTATIONS FROM FLANNERY O'CONNOR

What people don't realize is how much religion costs. They think faith is a big electric blanket, when of course it is the cross. It is much harder to believe than not to believe. If you feel you can't believe, you must at least do this: keep an open mind. Keep it open toward faith, keep wanting it, keep asking for it, and leave the rest to God.

———

Don't expect faith to clear things up for you. It is trust, not certainty . . .

———

Faith is a gift, but the will has a great deal to do with it. The loss of it is basically a failure of appetite, assisted by sterile intellect. Some people when they lose their faith in Christ, substitute a swollen faith in themselves.

———

I think that this experience you are having of losing your faith, or as you think, of having lost it, is an experience that in the long run belongs to faith; or at least it can belong to faith if faith is still valuable to you.[4]

LOST GLASSES

I woke up in the darkness and frantically searched for my glasses. They were not to be found. My myopic world closed in on me. Things that were previously seen at some distance were no longer visible; faces with once clearly defined features were now nothing but a blur; stars that pearled the night sky had disappeared.

Emily Dickinson begins one of her poems with the words "this world is not conclusion." Yet it has ended for those without the gift of faith. Being bound by time and space, confronted by the shadow of death, surrounded by suffering and anguish, it becomes difficult to believe in "the species that stands beyond." Fittingly the theologians and mystics speak about the *leap* of faith. This virtue allows us to fling ourselves into the trusting and providential arms of God without perceiving his presence.

Disbelief stalks our land. Whether we call it pessimism or cynicism, skepticism or despair—they all stem from a limited horizon and an inability or unwillingness to embrace a larger reality. Only faith opens new worlds. This grace comes as a gift and a task. Ultimately it is a relationship that connects us with a living and compassionate God.

Fortunately, by noon my glasses were found. Yet the morning's experience of blindness was invaluable. The lesson learned: how fragile the gifts of sight and faith—to be carefully nurtured and tended. During seasons and even years of disbelief there is one consolation—others have been there before us and, even if they were unable to find their glasses, someone came and took them by the hand. That touch gave them sight.

Greed

MANTRA: **The young man went away sad**

SOURCE: Matthew 19:16-22

Another time a man came up to him and said, "Teacher, what good must I do to possess everlasting life?" He answered, "Why do you question me about what is good? There is One who is good. If you wish to enter into life, keep the commandments." "Which ones?" he asked. Jesus replied, " 'You shall not kill'; 'You shall not commit adultery'; 'You shall not steal'; 'You shall not bear false witness'; 'Honor your father and your mother'; and 'Love your neighbor as yourself.' " The young man said to him, "I have kept all these; what do I need to do further?" Jesus told him, "If you seek perfection, go, sell your possessions, and give to the poor. You will then have treasure in heaven. Afterward, come back and follow me." Hearing these words, the young man went away sad, for his possessions were many.

PARALLEL REFERENCES

They devoted themselves to the apostles' instruction and the communal life, to the breaking of bread and the prayers. A reverent fear overtook them all, for many wonders and signs were performed by the apostles. Those who believed shared all things in common; they would sell their property and goods, dividing everything on the basis of each one's need.   *(Acts 2:42-45)*

There is, of course, great gain in religion — provided one is content with a sufficiency. We brought nothing into this world, nor have we the power to take anything out. If we have food and clothing we have all that we need. Those who want to be rich are falling into temptation and a trap. They are letting themselves be captured by foolish and harmful desires which drag men down to ruin and destruction. The love of money is the root of all evil. Some men in their passion for it have strayed from the faith, and have come to grief amid great pain.   *(1 Timothy 6:6-10)*

TOO MUCH IS NOT ENOUGH

THE YOUNG MAN WENT AWAY SAD,
THE YOUNG MAN WENT AWAY SAD

> back to the barns and cattle
> back to the cottage and the lake
> back to the portfolios and banquets

THE YOUNG MAN WENT AWAY SAD,
THE YOUNG MAN WENT AWAY SAD

> why give up a crown for a cross?
> why follow the narrow road?
> why surrender one's precious will?
> why trust the unknown with only a map in one's pocket?
> why risk losing one's life?

THE YOUNG MAN WENT AWAY SAD,
THE YOUNG MAN WENT AWAY SAD

> sad too the eyes of Jesus
> sad too the grieving Spirit
> sad too the empty embrace of the Father

THE YOUNG MAN WENT AWAY SAD,
THE YOUNG MAN WENT AWAY SAD.

The young man went a - way sad

PRAYER

Lord, you do not find room in an occupied heart. Empty us of ourselves and of things. Fill us with yourself. Apart from you is sadness. The land of greed is joyless. Come and make your home within us that our poverty might be filled. Grant this in your loving and tender mercy. *Amen.*

QUOTATIONS FROM MEISTER ECKHART

A man who is not satisfied with God is much too greedy. This, then, is the reward of all you do, that God knows about it and that through your deeds you aimed at him. Let that be enough. The more purely and simply you go out to him, the more thoroughly your deeds will wash your sins away.

———

Keep this in mind: to be full of things is to be empty of God, while to be empty of things is to be full of God.

———

Thus St. Augustine says: "The soul is greedy, to wish to know so much, and to have and hold it, and so, grasping for time, materiality and multiplicity, we lose what is uniquely our own." As long as (the spirit of "Give me") "More and More!" is in man, God can neither live nor work.

———

I have sometimes said that if a man goes seeking God and, with God, something else, he will not find God; but if one seeks only God—and really so—he will never find only God but along with God himself he will find all that God is capable of. If you seek your own advantage or blessing through God you are not really seeking God at all.[5]

THE WAY OF WHEY

In my grade school days one of my classmates would often invite me to stay over at his dad's farm. The motive was not entirely altruistic, since part of the invitation included helping him with his chores. In summer we would hay; in autumn, harvest the wheat; in early spring, cultivate the soil. Gathering eggs from the henhouse was a noisy business. But most interesting to me was feeding the hogs. As the whey was poured into the troughs these lumbering creatures would be transformed into a squealing mass, each fighting for its place at the dinner table, and within seconds everything was devoured.

The greed of the pigs brings home a lesson. There is an innate tendency in the animal and in the human world to fill up. Emptiness is abhorred — be it physical, psychological, or spiritual. At times, because the emptiness is so sharp and deep, almost anyone or anything will be taken in hopes of some satisfaction. To numb the hunger and quench the thirst is a constant longing.

Our Christian tradition provides a perspective for this tendency. For many it is a paradox and enigma. The call to poverty comes at the start of the beatitudes. The call to participate in the self-emptying *(kenosis)* of Jesus is grounded in our baptismal commitment. Greed is seen as a form of idolatry, an attempt to fill up on what is not God. Unfortunately the Gospel call is often not heeded, and the convergence on the troughs of life continues in forms of consumerism and over-indulgence.

The young man went away sad. Joylessness predominates unless we leave our hearts open to God. The price to be paid is high: silence and waiting. We must stand naked before the Lord and trust in his coming. The paradox will one day be resolved: our poverty becomes our richness, our emptiness fulfillment, our death new life.

Grief

MANTRA: **Your grief will be turned to joy**

SOURCE: John 16:20-22

I tell you truly:
you will weep and mourn
while the world rejoices;
you will grieve for a time,
but your grief will be turned to joy.
When a woman is in labor
she is sad that her time has come.
When she has borne her child,
she no longer remembers her pain
for joy that a man has been born into the world.
In the same way, you are sad for a time,
but I shall see you again;
then your hearts will rejoice
with a joy no one can take from you.

PARALLEL REFERENCES

I consider the sufferings of the present to be as nothing compared
with the glory to be revealed in us. Indeed, the whole created world
eagerly awaits the revelation of the sons of God. Creation was
made subject to futility, not of its own accord but by him who once
subjected it; yet not without hope, because the world itself will be
freed from its slavery to corruption and share in the glorious
freedom of the children of God. Yes, we know that all creation
groans and is in agony even until now. Not only that, but we

ourselves, although we have the Spirit as first fruits, groan inwardly while we await the redemption of our bodies. In hope we were saved. But hope is not hope if its object is seen; how is it possible for one to hope for what he sees? And hoping for what we cannot see means awaiting it with patient endurance.   *(Romans 8:18-25)*

Incline your ear, O LORD; answer me,
   for I am afflicted and poor.
Keep my life, for I am devoted to you;
   save your servant who trusts in you.
You are my God; have pity on me, O Lord,
   for to you I call all the day.
Gladden the soul of your servant,
   for to you, O Lord, I lift up my soul;
For you, O Lord, are good and forgiving,
   abounding in kindness to all who call upon you.
Hearken, O LORD, to my prayer
   and attend to the soul of my pleading.
In the day of my distress I call upon you,
   for you will answer me.
(Psalm 86:1-7)

A SINGLE COIN: GRIEF/JOY

YOUR GRIEF WILL BE TURNED TO JOY,
YOUR GRIEF WILL BE TURNED TO JOY

the spiral of grief and joy

the paradox of loss and gain
the enigma of death and life
the riddle of poverty and abundance
the maze of love and hate
the mystery of darkness and light

the spiral of grief and joy

the seed decaying that the rose might bloom
the anxiety of sin anointed with grace
the empty heart filled with the silence of love
the day yielding to the darkness of night
the tomb emptying into Easter joy

YOUR GRIEF WILL BE TURNED TO JOY,
YOUR GRIEF WILL BE TURNED TO JOY.

Your grief will be turned to joy

PRAYER

Lord God, we live in the cycle of woe and well-being. Help us to see
you in the darkness, to find your presence in all things. May the
sound of your voice at dusk give us courage to face the night; may
the dawn bring rejoicing. We ask only that you be with us in days
of grief and moments of joy. Without you our joy is empty, our
grief cannot be endured. Grant this in your love. *Amen.*

QUOTATIONS FROM THE POETS

And she replied: "There is no greater grief
Than to recall a bygone happiness
In present misery: that your teacher knows." *(Dante)*[6]

For friendly crowds that have long been dispersed.
My grief resounds to strangers, unknown throngs
Applaud it, and my anxious heart would burst.
Whoever used to praise my poem's worth,
If they still live, stray scattered through the earth. *(Goethe)*[7]

Some grief shows much of love;
But much of grief shows still some want of wit. *(Shakespeare)*[8]

THE PHONE CALL

While attending summer school at Notre Dame in 1970, I received a phone call telling of my father's heart attack. Within forty-eight hours he was dead, age sixty-six. In late October, 1975, another call came. My sister Joan, age forty, had been taken to the hospital. Within a day she died.

Sheer grief raced through the heart of our family. Although words of consolation and support of friends eased the pain somewhat, the grief remained. Each member of the family, having a unique relationship to a father and sister, husband and wife, walked the path of loss alone.

Midnight grief hungers for morning joy. Yet grief demands its own space and time. Dawn must not be forced; our grief must not be short-circuited. If it is, then its life cycle will simply return time and time again. The difficult challenge is to drink the dregs of grief to the bottom.

When death came to our family in 1970 and again in 1975, a friend of mine warned me about trying to escape the pain of loss. He noticed that I had become extremely active and busy, running from quiet and solitude. His advice was significant: look death in the face; remember all the details about your father and sister; embrace the hurt — then get on with life. Though initially resentful, I took the advice and am indebted to his wisdom.

The dawn will come. Death gives way to resurrection — this is our faith conviction. The great mystery of Christianity is focused in the Easter event. Sin and death have been conquered; their power has been broken. Yet we can get stuck in our grief. Our destination of joy is not assured unless we move on with hope. A large question arises: are we willing to live a life where our joys yield to grief, our griefs to joy? Are we willing to walk the human path that Jesus traveled?

Exile

MANTRA: **In the land of my exile**

SOURCE: Tobit 13:1-6

Then Tobit composed this joyful prayer:
  Blessed be God who lives forever,
    because his kingdom lasts for all ages,
  For he scourges and then has mercy;
    he casts down to the depths of the nether world,
    and he brings up from the great abyss.
  No one can escape his hand.

  Praise him, you Israelites, before the Gentiles,
    for though he has scattered you among them,
    he has shown you his greatness even there.
  Exalt him before every living being,
    because he is the Lord our God,
    our Father and God forever.

  He scourged you for your iniquities,
    but will again have mercy on you all.
  He will gather you from all the Gentiles
    among whom you have been scattered.

  When you turn back to him with all your heart,
    to do what is right before him,
  Then he will turn back to you,
    and no longer hide his face from you.

  So now consider what he has done for you,
    and praise him with full voice.

Bless the Lord of righteousness,
and exalt the King of the ages.

In the land of my exile I praise him
and show his power and majesty to a sinful nation.
"Turn back, you sinners! do the right before him!
perhaps he may look with favor upon you
and show you mercy."

PARALLEL REFERENCES

I will gather you from the nations and assemble you from the coun-
tries over which you have been scattered, and I will restore to you
the land of Israel. They shall return to it and remove from it all its
detestable abominations. I will give them a new heart and put a new
spirit within them; I will remove the stony heart from their bodies,
and replace it with a natural heart, so that they will live according
to my statutes, and observe and carry out my ordinances; thus they
shall be my people and I will be their God. But as for those whose
hearts are devoted to their detestable abominations, I will bring
down their conduct upon their heads, says the LORD GOD.

(Ezekiel 11:17-21)

"Give thanks to the LORD, for he is good,
for his kindness endures forever!"
Thus let the redeemed of the LORD say,
those whom he has redeemed from the hand of the foe
And gathered from the lands,
from the east and the west, from the north and the south.
They went astray in the desert wilderness;
the way to an inhabited city they did not find.
Hungry and thirsty,
their life was wasting away within them.
They cried to the LORD in their distress;
from their straits he rescued them.
And he led them by a direct way to reach an inhabited city,
Let them give thanks to the Lord for his kindness,
and his wondrous deeds to the children of men,
Because he satisfied the longing soul
and filled the hungry soul with good things. *(Psalm 107:1-9)*

AN EXILE'S SONG

IN THE LAND OF MY EXILE,
IN THE LAND OF MY EXILE . . .
  You came to find our broken hearts,
  You called through a gentle breeze,
  You died on a Friday we now call good.

IN THE LAND OF MY EXILE,
IN THE LAND OF MY EXILE . . .
> You tasted bitter, burning tears,
> You ate at our humble tables,
> You laughed and cried at early dawn.

IN THE LAND OF MY EXILE,
IN THE LAND OF MY EXILE . . .
> You found hands willing to serve,
> You slept in our stormy sterns,
> You climbed our craggy hills.

IN THE LAND OF MY EXILE,
IN THE LAND OF MY EXILE . . .
> You fell in love with May,
> You visited the darkness of midnight,
> You died and brought us home.

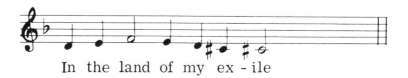

In the land of my ex - ile

PRAYER

Jesus, risen and living Lord, we praise you for coming to share in our exiled journey. Your love knew no bounds, your mercy felt no limits. Continue to draw us home and grace us that we might dream always of our homeland. Redeemer Lord, we thank you. *Amen.*

QUOTATIONS FROM CARL J. JUNG

I return now to the discovery I made in the course of associating with my rustic schoolmates. I found that they alienated me from myself. When I was with them I became different from the way I was at home.

In many cases in psychiatry, the patient who comes to us has a story that is not told, and which as a rule no one knows of. To my mind, therapy only really begins after the investigation of that wholly personal story. It is the patient's secret, the rock against which he is shattered. If I know this secret story, I have a key to the treatment. The doctor's task is to find out how to gain that knowledge. In most cases exploration of the conscious material is insufficient. Sometimes an association test can open the way; so can the interpretation of dreams, or long and patient human contact with the individual. In therapy the problem is always the whole person, never the symptom alone. We must ask questions which challenge the whole personality.

––––––

Loneliness does not come from having no people about one, but from being unable to communicate the things that seem important to oneself, or from holding certain views which others find inadmissible.

––––––

More than ever I wanted someone to talk with, but nowhere did I find a point of contact; on the contrary, I sensed in others an estrangement, a distrust, an apprehension which robbed me of speech.[9]

OUT OF WATER

They say fish feel no pain. Yet as the lake trout is cruelly torn from his home and landed in the bottom of the boat, something shudders through its body. Snatched from its home in the lake, it experiences distress. Then when measured and found wanting, the trout swims joyfully away, its exile ended.

Certain environments are familiar, others strange. To feel at home in a country or with a person is no small blessing. By contrast, the strangeness of a new culture, the disorientation felt in learning a new language, the experience of not belonging produce the exile-phenomenon. We are away from the climate or atmosphere of "at-homeness." Out of water and in the land of exile we suffer.

Teilhard's *The Divine Milieu* focuses on the faith-act that our
true home is in the presence of God. Yet we turn away from divine
light and love and enter the land of sin and darkness. Cut off from
the source of life we develop spiritual respiratory problems that are
fatal. Fullness of life is no longer possible. Such a self-chosen exile
is in need of a redeemer.

God is an "exile-ender." By means of reconciliation we are
brought home once again. Jesus comes to gather us as we stray
from the path of salvation. He comes to bring us to the divine banquet. He tastes our darkness and destroys it by his light. He plunges
into death to bring us resurrection. Our exile is ended, our lives
restored. Back in the baptismal water we swim our way home.

Tears

MANTRA: **Wipe every tear from their eyes**

SOURCE: Revelation 7:13-17

Then one of the elders asked me, "Who are these people all dressed in white? And where have they come from?" I said to him, "Sir, you should know better than I." He then told me, "These are the ones who have survived the great period of trial; they have washed their robes and made them white in the blood of the Lamb.

"It was this that brought them before God's throne:
    day and night they minister to him in his temple;
    he who sits on the throne will give them shelter.
Never again shall they know hunger or thirst,
    nor shall the sun or its heat beat down on them,
    for the Lamb on the throne will shepherd them.
He will lead them to springs of life-giving water,
    and God will wipe every tear from their eyes."

PARALLEL REFERENCES

When Mary came to the place where Jesus was, seeing him, she fell at his feet and said to him, "Lord, if you had been here my brother would never have died." When Jesus saw her weeping, and the Jews who had accompanied her also weeping, he was troubled in spirit, moved by the deepest emotions. "Where have you laid him?" he asked. "Lord, come and see," they said. Jesus began to weep, which caused the Jews to remark, "See how much he loved him!"
(John 11:32-36)

49

Coming within sight of the city, he wept over it and said: "If only you had known the path to peace this day; but you have completely lost it from view!"   *(Luke 19:41-42)*

Wipe ev-ery tear from their eyes

RIVERS OF PAIN

WIPE EVERY TEAR FROM THEIR EYES,
WIPE EVERY TEAR FROM THEIR EYES
The refugee
— without home
— without possessions
— without acceptance

WIPE EVERY TEAR FROM THEIR EYES,
WIPE EVERY TEAR FROM THEIR EYES
The abandoned parent
— locked away in fear
— forgotten by family and friends
— facing death alone

WIPE EVERY TEAR FROM THEIR EYES,
WIPE EVERY TEAR FROM THEIR EYES
The abused child
— beaten in word and deed
— bruised by silence and neglect
— unwanted and scorned

WIPE EVERY TEAR FROM THEIR EYES,
WIPE EVERY TEAR FROM THEIR EYES
with your mercy, Lord, wipe away our sins
with your peace, Lord, wipe away our chaos
with your gentleness, Lord, wipe away our violence.

Wipe ev - ery tear from their eyes

PRAYER

Gracious and loving Father, our tears are many. They form a river
of pain, they cry out for healing. Through Jesus, wipe away every
tear from our eyes that we might rejoice in your kingdom of love
and peace, justice, and freedom. Grant this through him who wept
for us. *Amen.*

QUOTATIONS FROM ANNE FRANK

The sun is shining, the sky is a deep blue, there is a lovely breeze and I'm longing—so longing—for everything. To talk, for freedom, for friends, to be alone. And I do so long . . . to cry! I feel as if I'm going to burst, and I know that it would get better with crying; but I can't, I'm restless, I go from one room to the other, breathe through the crack of a closed window, feel my heart beating, as if it is saying, "Can't you satisfy my longings at last?"

I believe that it's spring within me, I feel that spring is awakening, I feel it in my whole body and soul. It is an effort to behave normally, I feel utterly confused, don't know what to read, what to write, what to do, I only know that I am longing . . . !

––––––

The best remedy for those who are afraid, lonely, or unhappy is to go outside, somewhere where they can be quite alone with the heavens, nature, and God. Because only then does one feel that all is as it should be and that God wishes to see people happy, amidst the simple beauty of nature. As long as this exists, and it certainly always will, I know that then there will always be comfort for every sorrow, whatever the circumstances may be. And I firmly believe that nature brings solace in all troubles.

––––––

I want to go on living even after my death! And therefore I am grateful to God for giving me this gift, this possibility of developing myself and of writing, of expressing all that is in me.[10]

CROCODILE TEARS

Although I have been to the zoo many times and have seen hundreds of alligators and crocodiles, I have never seen a crocodile cry. Perhaps that is why crocodile tears are mere fable. However, among us humans tears can be real and abundant.

Human tears come in different intensities and in diverse seasons: tears of a small child who stubs his toe; tears of a mother who has lost her son; tears of greeting after years of separation; tears of a winter day, frozen on the cheek; tears of a penitent blessed with God's mercy. Where tears are shed the Lord is present.

From what distant stream do tears arise? Certainly from some subterranean river that lies close to the heart. Some call it the river of Compassion, others the river of Mercy or Forgiveness. At times of loss and suffering, at times of extreme joy and humor the river overflows and our eyes and faces are washed clean once again. How tragic were that river to dry up!

In their concern for good vision, optometrists give people a thorough check-up. Many areas are the object of concern: peripheral vision, ability to focus, blind spots, depth perception — and tear-flow. Without moisture to the eyes our vision can be impaired. Without moisture from our heart, life becomes hard and bitter.

How fitting it is that we enter the Christian community through baptismal water. Though we draw it from our own wells and bless it ourselves, the water ultimately comes from God. Could that water be his tears?

Weakness

MANTRA: **I am content with weakness**

SOURCE: 2 Corinthians 12:7-10

But I refrain, lest anyone think more of me than what he sees in me or hears from my lips. As to the extraordinary revelations, in order that I might not become conceited I was given a thorn in the flesh, an angel of Satan to beat me and keep me from getting proud. Three times I begged the Lord that this might leave me. He said to me, "My grace is enough for you, for in weakness power reaches perfection." And so I willingly boast of my weaknesses instead, that the power of Christ may rest upon me.

Therefore I am content with weakness, with mistreatment, with distress, with persecutions and difficulties for the sake of Christ; for when I am powerless, it is then that I am strong.

PARALLEL REFERENCES

Do you not know or have you not heard?
The LORD is the eternal God, creator of the ends of the earth.
He does not faint nor grow weary, and his knowledge is beyond
    scrutiny.
He gives strength to the fainting; for the weak he makes vigor
    abound.   *(Isaiah 40:28-29)*

All through this, Simon Peter had been standing there warming himself. They said to him, "Are not you a disciple of his?" He denied it and said, "I am not!" "But did I not see you with him in the garden?" insisted one of the high priest's slaves—as it happened, a relative of the man whose ear Peter had severed. Peter denied it again. At that moment a cock began to crow.

(John 18:25-27)

THE WEAK LINK IN THE CHAIN

I AM CONTENT WITH WEAKNESS,
I AM CONTENT WITH WEAKNESS

that is—

    if my failure really hides success
    if personal faults go unnoticed by others
    if my shame is not revealed in a blush
    if the crown promised comes without the cross

I AM CONTENT WITH WEAKNESS,
I AM CONTENT WITH WEAKNESS

that is—

    if no one else is successful
    if no scorn or ridicule follow
    if pain be but transitory and short
    if other people hold it in admiration

I AM CONTENT WITH WEAKNESS,
I AM CONTENT WITH WEAKNESS.

I am con-tent with weak-ness

PRAYER

God of humility, draw us into the truth of who we really are—totally and completely dependent upon you. In our weakness, be our strength; in our darkness, be our light; in our discouragement, be our hope. Then all weakness can be embraced. Deepen within our hearts the sense of your presence, for in it we find all strength. Grant this through our risen Lord. *Amen.*

QUOTATIONS FROM ROMANO GUARDINI

Often, naively, we imagine the illumination of a prophet as a fixed thing, as though he had only to behold, once, in order to know without wavering forever after; as though once gripped by the

Spirit, he stood fast for all time. In reality even a prophet's life is shaken by all storms and saddled with all weaknesses.

It seems that upon entering the world, God renounced his omnipotence; he, Truth, left his mantle of irresistibility outside the gates of earth, in order to enter in a form that would permit people to close their hearts to him if they so desired. Purposely God limited his illimitable radiance, wrapping himself in a darkness which enabled men to withstand and even to reject his rays. Perhaps in imposing these limitations on himself, God was conforming to the weakness of the creatures to whom he descended.

God is lord of the world and men, but his manner of entering the world and approaching men is not that of a Lord. The moment he descends to earth he becomes mysteriously weak. It is as though he has left his omnipotence outside the gates of his human existence. Once in the world, its forces seem stronger than he, seem to justify themselves against him.[11]

MEMORIES ARE MADE OF THIS

In the back regions of my memory I recall some reflections that a math teacher offered us seniors on a lazy spring day. Our teacher loved philosophy more than abstract figures and often he would venture off on some back road of thought and share random reflections. Snatches come back to me from this peripatetic: "Remember, it's important to have a good self-image . . . this will mean that you get in touch with your gifts; it will also mean that we get in touch with our weakness . . . strange to say, it happens sometimes that our strengths become our weakness, our weakness becomes our greatest asset . . . one example from my own life might be helpful: I have always loved public speaking and basically I'm good at it . . . but one day I began to panic over the fear of failure . . . if a talk did not go exceedingly well I would become despondent and upset . . . I had grown to identify with the gift so much that it controlled my life . . . on the other side of the coin: I would often make a promise or commitment and fail to follow through, thus disappointing many people, including myself . . . eventually a friend confronted me on this with some hard facts accusing me of irresponsibility and infidelity . . . the truth hit home and I had to make some radical changes in my life's journey . . . I came to learn the seriousness of giving one's word: my weakness elicited from my friend an honesty that shocked me to the bone . . . I leave you with but one thought: don't be fooled by apparent strengths, don't be overwhelmed by your weakness . . . each has its advantages and pitfalls."

I know few people who are content with weakness; most desire to be strong and in control—including myself. Saint Paul must have been far down the spiritual road in his contentment with weakness. Hopefully this was not bravado. At any rate, the lesson has been given . . . by distant saints, philosophic math teachers, life itself.

Abandonment

MANTRA: **Everyone abandoned me**

SOURCE: 2 Timothy 4:14-18

Alexander the coppersmith did me a great deal of harm; the Lord will repay him according to his deeds. Meanwhile, you too had better be on guard, for he has strongly resisted our preaching. At the first hearing of my case in court, no one took my part. In fact, everyone abandoned me. May it not be held against them! But the Lord stood by my side and gave me strength, so that through me the preaching task might be completed and all the nations might hear the gospel. That is how I was saved from the lion's jaws. The Lord will continue to rescue me from all attempts to do me harm and will bring me safe to his heavenly kingdom. To him be glory forever and ever. *Amen.*

PARALLEL REFERENCES

They [Joseph's brothers] then sat down to their meal. Looking up, they saw a caravan of Ishmaelites coming from Gilead, their camels laden with gum, balm and resin to be taken down to Egypt. Judah said to his brothers: "What is to be gained by killing our brother and concealing his blood? Rather, let us sell him to these Ishmaelites, instead of doing away with him ourselves. After all, he is our brother, our own flesh." His brothers agreed. They sold Joseph to the Ishmaelites for twenty pieces of silver.

(Genesis 37:25-28)

My couch is among the dead,
like the slain who lie in the grave,

Whom you remember no longer
and who are cut off from your care.
You have plunged me into the bottom of the pit,
into the dark abyss.
Upon me your wrath lies heavy,
and with all your billows you overwhelm me.

(Psalm 88:6-8)

THE STRANDED

EVERYONE ABANDONED ME,
EVERYONE ABANDONED ME—

> the early morning sun ran behind the clouds
> the harvest moon dropped off the western sky
> the ground hog refused to cast his shadow
> an unkind wind swept away the August butterflies
> the river surrendered itself to the thirsty earth

EVERYONE ABANDONED ME,
EVERYONE ABANDONED ME—

> yesterday's joys on an extended vacation
> last summer's hope swallowed up in despair
> creative thoughts frozen in the mind's dormant field
> memories of youth blocked by hardening arteries
> noble deeds aborted by persistent fears

EVERYONE ABANDONED ME,
EVERYONE ABANDONED ME—

> the poets: unable to speak my dreams
> the mystics: unable to enter my small world
> the scientists: unable to touch my mystery
> the doctors: unable to embrace my pain
> the innocent: unable to understand my sin

EVERYONE ABANDONED ME,
EVERYONE ABANDONED ME.

Ev - ery - one a - ban - doned me

PRAYER

Your word tells, Lord, that you will never forget or abandon us.
Yet so many experiences seem to exclude your presence. Heal my

blindness that I might see you in all events. You are faithful; you are near. In my sense of abandonment bring your consolation. We ask this in Jesus, who himself experienced abandonment. *Amen.*

QUOTATIONS FROM THOMAS MERTON

And by receiving His will with joy and doing it with gladness I have His love in my heart, because my will is now the same as His love and I am on the way to becoming what He is, Who is Love. And by accepting all things from Him I receive His joy into my soul, not because things are what they are but because God is Who He is, and His love has willed my joy in them all.

_____

. . . the simplest definition of freedom is this: it means the ability to do the will of God. To be able to resist His will is not to be free. In sin there is no true freedom.

_____

The secret of interior peace is detachment.

_____

For when our minds and wills are perfectly free from every created attachment, they are immediately perfectly filled with the gift of God's love: not because things necessarily have to happen that way, but because this is His will, the gift of His love to us.[12]

HIGH AND DRY

The fears of life are many. Though the fear of abandonment is not necessarily at the top, it is high on the list. Anxiety about being left behind with the responsibility and aloneness that that entails can be overwhelming. Surprising is the fact that so many people do survive, that some have even excelled despite this plight.

Her name was Catherine. By age twelve she was an orphan. Her parents, taken away by untimely deaths, left her alone in a large world. Gradually her children moved away and then, when she was sixty-seven, her husband died suddenly, leaving her all alone. On both ends of life the abandonment faced her with all the accompanying anguish, sense of loss and fear.

Two basic human needs are threatened by the experience of abandonment: belonging and meaning. The hunger to be part of a group and in close relationship is powerful and deep. Not to be wanted as children is one way of getting our names on the "most wanted" list. Are not all the noted criminals deprived of this need in their childhood? Cut adrift in the ocean of life without any reference point incapacitates the human spirit. The other need is for meaning. Since meaning is ultimately relational—being in relationship with others—no amount of cognitive wisdom can satiate this need. Abandonment strips the heart of meaning and leaves the mind without perspective.

The orphan and the widow—paradigms of abandonment. Yet reality has a harsher note—sometimes abandonment comes not from death but from the voluntary choice of another. Freely to walk away from human bonding, for whatever reason, is a frontal attack on belonging and meaning. After such an experience one has to wonder if trust will ever again be possible.

Fear, "the malignant disease of the what-if's," has many victims. But included in all fear, fear of water, fear of crowds, fear of death, is the fear of abandonment. Faith hopefully intervenes: "I will never leave you"—words of God promising fidelity.

Darkness

MANTRA: **My only friend is darkness**

SOURCE: Psalm 88:14-19

But I, O LORD, cry out to you;
  with my morning prayer I wait upon you.
Why, O LORD, do you reject me;
  why hide from me your face?
I am afflicted and in agony from my youth;
  I am dazed with the burden of your dread.
Your furies have swept over me;
  your terrors have cut me off.
They encompass me like water all the day;
  on all sides they close in upon me.
Companion and neighbor you have taken away from me;
  my only friend is darkness.

PARALLEL REFERENCES

My soul ebbs away from me;
  days of affliction have overtaken me.
My frame takes no rest by night;
  my inward parts seethe and will not be stilled.
I go about in gloom, without the sun;
  I rise up in public to voice my grief. *(Job 30:27-28)*

I am a man who knows affliction from the rod of his anger,
One whom he has led and forced to walk in darkness, not in the
  light;

Against me alone he brings back his hand again and again all the
day.

(Lamentations 3:1-3)

FRIENDLY DARKNESS

MY ONLY FRIEND IS DARKNESS,
MY ONLY FRIEND IS DARKNESS:

the shadows of ambiguity
the nameless fears in the valley
the lingering guilt of stolen apples
the shaggy and pursuant melancholy
the threatening avalanche of ridicule

MY ONLY FRIEND IS DARKNESS,
MY ONLY FRIEND IS DARKNESS:

the violent volcano of anger
　　the hidden iceberg of jealousy and lust
　　　　the tortuous path of discouragement
　　　　　　the defective seeds of failure
　　　　　　　　the deepening silence of old age

MY ONLY FRIEND IS DARKNESS,
MY ONLY FRIEND IS DARKNESS.

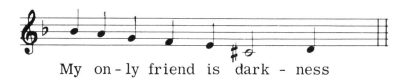

My　on-ly　friend　is　dark - ness

PRAYER

God of light and darkness, you come to us in the brightness of the noonday sun and in the haunting time of midnight. When we walk in darkness and pain, manifest your presence. If we are unable to see, guide us in the darkness by means of faith and hope. Befriend us in the darkness with your quiet love. Send your Spirit of peace. *Amen.*

QUOTATIONS FROM WILLIAM STYRON

I now could not even recall when the ability to pray had left me—one month, two months, perhaps even more. It might have been some consolation, at least, had I known the reason why this power had deserted me; but I was denied even this knowledge and there seemed no way at all to bridge the gulf between myself and God.

"Ah, what bitter tears God must weep at the sight of the things that men do to other men!" He broke off then and I saw him shake his head convulsively, his voice a sudden cry: "In the name of money! *Money!*"

———

It had been my custom for many years, as I have said before, to spend part of this hour of the day in prayer and meditation, but when I went back to the border of the woods and knelt there to ask God's guidance in the coming time of solitude—to request that He show me the ways and necessities for my salvation now that my cause in His name was irrevocably lost—I found to my terrible distress that for the first time in my life I was unable even to think. Try as I might, I could not cause a prayer to pass my lips. The God I knew was slipping away from me. And I lingered there in the early morning and felt as alone and as forsaken as I had ever felt since I had learned God's name.[13]

"NOW CRACKS A NOBLE HEART"

In the darkness of the night, the dead King Hamlet speaks to his son, the prince. As the tragedy of his father's death is revealed to him, the young Prince Hamlet experiences the physical darkness of midnight turning into a psychological darkness of despair. With the loss of light he begins to walk the dark path of madness. Abandoned by friends, betrayed by his mother, deceived by his incestuous uncle, seemingly rejected by the beautiful Ophelia, Hamlet's only friend is darkness.

For years scholars have puzzled over Hamlet's real or feigned insanity. Although lacking clarity on this question, we can understand the pain his heart endured. So severe was the suffering that even the sage advice of friends could not penetrate the darkness. The haunting soliloquies, so brilliant in insight and eloquence, have spoken to many human hearts that travel similar paths.

Darkness, like the ocean, is vast and mysterious. Its stormy nature and midnight quality cause confusion in the grasping human mind and sensitive heart. At times only endurance comes as a possible response. Inadequate as it is, sometimes it is the only option. One of the Hebrew psalms tells that with the dawn there will be rejoicing; once the darkness breaks, the light will come. Yet in the center of the storm the very existence of the sun is called into doubt.

For Hamlet, caught in tragedy, everything else seemed unreal. His subjective state controlled the boundaries of his inner and outer world. For him in this situation only darkness could be called a friend. Yet reality is larger than our perception or felt experience. Darkness does not define reality. Midnight cannot claim that the noontime implies nonexistence. Shakespeare's play challenges us to examine the very nature of reality.

Noble hearts do crack. Health, at every level, is easily lost. But hearts are also strong and life resilient. The darkness comes for its untimely visitation; light also is given in and through the cracks.

II.
Midnight Mantras
and the Mystics

Melancholy

MANTRA: **Its tinge of melancholy**

SOURCE: *Story of a Soul: The Autobiography of St. Thérèse of Lisieux*

I return once more to my Sundays. This *joyous* day, passing all too quickly, had its tinge of *melancholy.* I remember how my happiness was unmixed until Compline. During this prayer, I would begin thinking that the day of *rest* was coming to an end, that the morrow would bring with it the necessity of beginning life over again, we would have to go back to work, to learning lessons, etc., and my heart felt the *exile* of this earth. I longed for the everlasting repose of heaven, that never-ending *Sunday* of the *Fatherland.*[14]

PARALLEL REFERENCES

Hear, O God, my cry; listen to my prayer!
From the earth's end I call to you as my heart grows faint.
You will set me high upon a rock; you will give me rest,
    for you are my refuge, a tower of strength against the enemy.
Oh, that I might lodge in your tent forever,
    take refuge in the shelter of your wings!

You indeed, O God, have accepted my vows;
    you granted me the heritage of those who fear your name.
Add to the days of the king's life; let his years be many generations;
Let him sit enthroned before God forever;
    bid kindness and faithfulness preserve him.
So I will sing the praises of your name forever,
    fulfilling my vows day by day. *(Psalm 61)*

"Do not let your hearts be troubled.
Have faith in God and faith in me.
In my Father's house there are many dwelling places;
otherwise, how could I have told you that I was going to prepare a
    place for you?
I am indeed going to prepare a place for you,
    and then I shall come back to take you with me,
    that where I am you also may be.
You know the way that leads where I go." *(John 14:1-4)*

Its tinge of mel - an - chol - y

MELANCHOLIC MOOD

ITS TINGE OF MELANCHOLY

A rainy dark October day,
Leaves, once green, now peacock-hued,
Geese abandoning northern homes for a safer, warmer south,
The sun, turned shy, leaving earlier each evening,
Churning winds jarring the silent sounds of night.

An inner turmoil of darkness and confusion,
Safe beliefs confronted by doubt and fear,
Friends gone to distant lands, new worlds,
Even God's light and love, fallen off the world,
Melancholy now a way of life, not a season.

What has been lost—what is missing?
Fruit-filled trees? Sunlit skies? A gentle breeze? Brilliant new
    insights?
Sure knowledge? Faithful friends? Peaceful order?
All this and much more—an unnamed something/Someone . . .
A subtle, personal hope . . . please come.

ITS TINGE OF MELANCHOLY

PRAYER

Lord, grace us with your hope and joy. Fill our emptiness with your
peace and presence. So often we taste the abyss of loneliness and
seek to fill it with things and schedules. Each day renew your love
in our hearts; do not abandon us to the darkness. You are our
hope, our joy, our peace. *Amen.*

QUOTATIONS FROM WILLIAM JAMES

It all depends on how sensitive the soul may become to discords. "The trouble with me is that I believe too much in common happiness and goodness," said a friend of mine whose consciousness was of this sort, "and nothing can console me for their transiency. I am appalled and disconcerted at its being possible." And so with most of us: a little cooling down of animal excitability and instinct, a little loss of animal toughness, a little irritable weakness and descent of the pain-threshold, will bring the worm at the core of all our usual springs of delight into full view, and turn us into melancholy metaphysicians.

———

In his instructive work, la Tristesse et la Joie, M. Georges Dumas compares together the melancholy and the joyous phase of circular insanity, and shows that, while selfishness characterizes the one, the other is marked by altruistic impulses.

———

One can never fathom an emotion or divine its dictates by standing outside it. In the glowing hour of excitement, however, all incomprehensibilities are solved, and what was so enigmatical from without becomes transparently obvious.[15]

"THE MOON NEVER BEAMS . . ."

It was in midwinter. Basketball practice was over and I was working my way home through the early dusk. My homework tucked under my arm, my body tired from a strenuous workout, I suddenly became aware of the full moon rising in the eastern sky. Something turned over in my sophomore heart—something haunting, something yearning, something wistful. Since that time the moon has always brought me back home to my deep-seated melancholy.

Within that experience, at its core and center, is the consciousness that "something is missing." Was it once had and lost? Was it ever within one's possession? These questions are too academic. The immediacy of the incompleteness of life, the insatiable hunger and thirst for fullness of life, the dread of emptiness—all of these vultures encircle the soul. Such experiences come and go, they are found in every season and place. Suddenly they break in upon us reminding us of the finitude of our lives and the shortness of the journey.

Melancholy contains a secret grace. It pulls us into the beyond, out of reach of more immediate fulfillment. It reminds us that there is transcendence in life, that something very deep will never be satisfied with surface realities. At times it comes as a nudge and nibble, at other times like a jolt or bolt of lightning. Avoidance is one response but even our compensations quickly run dry. The bucket has a hole which only a plunge into the ocean can fill.

Melancholy has a dark side—it can cause paralysis: physical, moral, spiritual. Without hope, people close up their tent early on life. No event or person can adequately fill the void. Here only a religious conviction that moves beyond the finitude of life and the finality of death provides that desire with expectation that we label hope. The challenge will always be to befriend melancholy and not allow it to become an enemy. Then her companionship can teach us many valuable lessons.

Waiting

MANTRA: **We wait for him steadfastly**

SOURCE: *Showings* by Julian of Norwich

It is God's will that we receive three things from him as gifts as we seek. The first is that we seek willingly and diligently without sloth, as that may be with his grace, joyfully and happily, without unreasonable depression and useless sorrow. The second is that we wait for him steadfastly, out of love for him, without grumbling and contending against him, to the end of our lives, for that will last only for a time. The third is that we have great trust in him, out of complete and true faith, for it is his will that we know that he will appear, suddenly and blessedly, to all his lovers. For he works in secret, and he will be perceived, and his appearing will be very sudden. And he wants to be trusted, for he is very accessible, familiar and courteous, blessed may he be.[16]

PARALLEL REFERENCES

Then Job answered the LORD and said:
> I know that you can do all things, and that no purpose of
> yours can be hindered.
> I have dealt with great things that I do not understand;
> > things too wonderful for me, which I cannot know.
> I had heard of you by word of mouth, but now my eye has seen
> you.
> Therefore I disown what I have said, and repent in dust and
> ashes. *(Job 42:1-6)*

There was also a certain prophetess, Anna by name, daughter of Phanuel of the tribe of Asher. She had seen many days, having lived seven years with her husband after her marriage and then as a widow until she was eighty-four. She was constantly in the temple, worshiping day and night in fasting and prayer. Coming on the scene at this moment, she gave thanks to God and talked about the child to all who looked forward to the deliverance of Jerusalem.

(Luke 2:36-38)

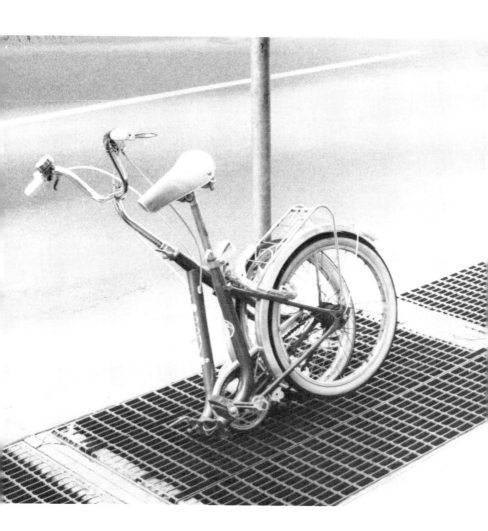

STEADFAST WAITING

WE WAIT FOR HIM STEADFASTLY,
WE WAIT FOR HIM STEADFASTLY.

In darkened woods—the way lost,
On river banks—in painful emptiness,
On cold mountain peaks—mist-covered and lonely,
In crowded rooms—afraid and in doubt.

WE WAIT FOR HIM STEADFASTLY,
WE WAIT FOR HIM STEADFASTLY.

At dawn—with great expectation,
At noon—with joy-filled jubilation,
At dusk—with sunset exaltation,
At midnight—with courageous anticipation.

WE WAIT FOR HIM STEADFASTLY,
WE WAIT FOR HIM STEADFASTLY.

When a friend dies—the heart is broken,
When memory fades—timelines vanish,
When the mugger strikes—trust vaporizes,
When anger kills—poison spreads.

WE WAIT FOR HIM STEADFASTLY,
WE WAIT FOR HIM STEADFASTLY.

We wait for him stead - fast - ly

PRAYER

Father of all time and space, we await your coming with hope and fear. Do not abandon us to darkness or to ourselves. Send the light of your love, bestow the gift of your peace, reside in our hearts. Filled with your presence we will build the oneness that you desire. Patient and loving God, come to our aid. *Amen.*

QUOTATIONS FROM JOHN HENRY NEWMAN

. . . they felt the weariness of waiting, and the sickness of delayed hope, and did not understand that I was as perplexed as they were, and, being of more sensitive complexion of mind than myself, were made ill by the suspense.

―――――

There is a time for every thing, and many a man desires a reformation of an abuse, or the fuller development of a doctrine, or the adoption of a particular policy, but forgets to ask himself whether the right time for it is come; and, knowing that there is no one who will be doing anything towards its accomplishment in his own lifetime unless he does it himself, he will not listen to the voice of authority, and he spoils a good work in his own century, in order that another man, as yet unborn, may not have the opportunity of bringing it happily to perfection in the next.[17]

―――――

The moment before acting may be, as can easily be imagined, peculiarly dreary—the mind may be confused—no reason for acting may be forthcoming in our mind—and the awful greatness of the step in itself, and without any distinct apprehension of its consequences, may weigh on us. Some persons like to be left to themselves in such a crisis—others find comfort in the presence of others—I could do nothing but shut myself in my room and lie on my bed.[18]

SUNRISE

Three hours beyond midnight I climbed the sandbank high above Lake Michigan. There I set up my lawn chair and wrapped myself in a June blanket. My self-assigned task was to wait for the sunrise—hopefully with patience.

The first half hour went well; I was alert and vigilant. Gradually, however, my eyes grew weary and sought rest in more sleep. The temptation was victorious and I dozed. Around 4:15 A.M. I was startled awake by an inconsiderate bird who decided, without consultation—at least from me—to greet the dawn. The sky was illuminated with the rays of dawn chasing the darkness deeper into the west. In deep disappointment I tasted my infidelity to the original plan. I had missed the sunrise.

But then my apparent failure gave way to joy. Like a mouse peeking out of its hiding place, the orange ball crept over the horizon of the lake with majesty and dignity. It burst upon the sand and all its inhabitants. Though undeserving, I, too, was showered with the graced rays.

Waiting for the sunrise carries the same emotion as waiting for a letter to come, the phone to ring, the guest to arrive. Such is a basic fact of our human condition. In that waiting there is often great pain and suffering, since it involves fear of disappointment or abandonment. Some individuals experience this kind of poverty their whole lifetime.

Fortunately most of us are graciously surprised by letters, calls, and friends. Yet in the waiting there are lessons: the letter not arrived creates space to reflect upon the gift of friendship; the silent phone challenges us to reach out to others lest they experience abandonment; the tardy guest calls us to ever-deeper hospitality. Waiting can be a holy time offering redemption.

I have not gotten up for a sunrise for a long time now. My ability to wait is dull and insensitive. More practice—and less sleep—may be in order.

Sin

MANTRA: **There is no darker darkness**

SOURCE: Teresa of Avila's *The Interior Castle*

Before going on I want to say that you should consider what it would mean to this so brilliantly shining and beautiful castle, this pearl from the Orient, this tree of life planted in the very living waters of life — that is, in God — to fall into mortal sin; there's no darker darkness nor anything more obscure and black. You shouldn't want to know anything else than the fact that, although the very sun that gave the soul so much brilliance and beauty is still in the center, the soul is as though it were not there to share in these things. Yet it is as capable of enjoying His Majesty as is crystal capable of reflecting the sun's brilliance. Nothing helps such a soul, and as a result all the good works it might do while in mortal sin are fruitless for the attainment of glory. Since these works do not proceed from that principle, which is God, who is the cause of our virtue's being really virtue, and are separated from Him, they cannot be pleasing in His sight. Since, after all, the intention of anyone who commits a mortal sin is to please the devil, not God, the poor soul becomes darkness itself because the devil is darkness itself.[19]

PARALLEL REFERENCES

There was a time when you were darkness, but now you are light in the Lord. Well then, live as children of light. Light produces every kind of goodness and justice and truth. Be correct in your judgment of what pleases the Lord. Take no part in vain deeds done in darkness; rather, condemn them. It is shameful even to mention the

things these people do in secret; but when such deeds are con-
demned they are seen in the light of day, and all that then appears is
light. *(Ephesians 5:8-13)*

As he walked along, he saw a man who had been blind from birth.
His disciples asked him, "Rabbi, was it his sin or that of his parents
that caused him to be born blind?" "Neither," answered Jesus: "It
was no sin, either of this man or of his parents. Rather, it was to let
God's works show forth in him. We must do the deeds of him who
sent me while it is day. The night comes on when no one can work.
While I am in the world I am the light of the world." *(John 9:1-5)*

DARKEST DARKNESS

THERE IS NO DARKER DARKNESS,
THERE IS NO DARKER DARKNESS

      . . . than to turn one's back on God
      . . . than to leave the land one loves
      . . . than to forget the house of grace
      . . . than to misuse the gift of freedom
      . . . than to mar the pearl of faith

THERE IS NO DARKER DARKNESS,
THERE IS NO DARKER DARKNESS

      . . . than to shatter fragile innocence
      . . . than to squelch the hope of the young
      . . . than to waste the gift of time
      . . . than to betray a friend's embrace
      . . . than to despair of any change

THERE IS NO DARKER DARKNESS,
THERE IS NO DARKER DARKNESS.

There is no dark - er dark - ness

PRAYER

Lord of grace and love, when we turn from you we walk in the
darkness of sin. Bring us back to the embrace of your love. Send
your Spirit to transform our minds and hearts, to convert our wills.
Forgive our sins, heal our divisions, let us rejoice in your gentle and
tender mercy. Grant this in your love, Jesus. *Amen.*

QUOTATIONS FROM CATHERINE OF SIENA

For there is no sin that does not touch others, whether secretly by refusing them what is due them, or openly by giving birth to the vices of which I have told you.

———

For if self-knowledge and the thought of sin are not seasoned with remembrance of the blood and hope for mercy, the result is bound to be confusion.

———

. . . for they cannot abuse themselves without abusing their neighbors. If they abuse themselves by sinning, they are abusing the souls of their neighbors.

———

. . . for I told you that every sin as well as every virtue is realized through your neighbors. Sin is committed through lack of charity for God and your neighbors, and virtue is practiced out of the warmth of charity.[20]

THE KING'S SIN

King David had sinned. His trespasses: murder and adultery. Nathan the prophet was sent by God to call the king to conversion. Though in darkness, the king felt the blinding light of Nathan's word and turned back to the Lord. The journey through guilt and shame was torturous but necessary; the darkness finally led to light.

Another king, Claudius by name, appears in Shakespeare's *Hamlet.* His sin was similar to that of David—murder, ambition, seeking another man's wife. Claudius utters a profound theological insight. To move from the darkness of sin one has to give up the consequences of sin. Unwillingness to do so means that forgiveness remains inaccessible:

> My fault is past. But, O! what form
>   of prayer
> Can serve my turn? 'Forgive me my
>   foul murder?'
> That cannot be since I am still
>   possess'd
> Of those effects for which I did the
>   murder,
> My crown, mine own ambition, and
>   my queen.
> May one be pardon'd and retain the
>   offence?[21]

Darkness comes in different degrees but ultimately the darkness caused by sin returns to misuse freedom. Choices are made that cause division and alienation within relationships. Creatures are used as means to an end; manipulation and exploitation become ways of life; self-serving tendencies are expressed without regard for the well-being of others. Darker and darker becomes this dreadful night.

And yet grace abounds even more than sin. The Lord does not leave us in the dark but sends other Nathans and interior nudgings to move us to the light of grace. The Lord desires that we live in peace, in oneness, and harmony. Underlying the love motif behind the incarnation, redemption, and resurrection is that longing that all people one day share in the eternal banquet. God would go to and through the cross to achieve this divine desire. The cross, seemingly so dark, becomes our light. It is the free act that brings liberation for all.

David sinned and fell into darkness. Jesus, our risen king, comes as the light of the world. There is no greater light than he.

Ambiguity

MANTRA: **In this cloud of unknowing**

SOURCE: *The Cloud of Unknowing*

In the lower degree of the active life a person does well to busy himself with good deeds and the works of mercy. In the higher degree of the active life (which merges with the lower degree of the contemplative life) he begins to meditate on the things of the spirit. This is when he ought to ponder with sorrow the sinfulness of man so as to enter into the Passion of Christ and the sufferings of his saints with pity and compassion. It is a time when one grows in appreciation of God's kindness and his gifts, and begins to praise and thank him for the wonderful ways he works in all his creation. But in the higher degree of contemplation — such as we know it in this life — all is darkness and a *cloud of unknowing*. Here one turns to God with a burning desire for himself alone and rests in the blind awareness of his naked being.[22]

PARALLEL REFERENCES

I must go on boasting, however useless it may be, and speak of visions and revelations of the Lord. I know a man in Christ who, fourteen years ago, whether he was in or outside his body I cannot say, only God can say — a man who was snatched up to the third heaven. I know that this man — whether in or outside his body I do not know, God knows — was snatched up to Paradise to hear words which cannot be uttered, words which no man may speak. About this man I will boast; but I will do no boasting about myself unless it be about my weaknesses. And even if I were to boast it would not be folly in me because I would only be telling the truth. *(2 Cor. 12:1-6)*

Six days later, Jesus took Peter, James, and John off by themselves with him and led them up a high mountain. He was transfigured before their eyes and his clothes became dazzlingly white — whiter than the work of any bleacher could make them. Elijah appeared to them along with Moses; the two were in conversation with Jesus. Then Peter spoke to Jesus: "Rabbi, how good it is for us to be here! Let us erect three booths on this site, one for you, one for Moses, and one for Elijah." He hardly knew what to say, for they were all overcome with awe. A cloud came, overshadowing them, and out of the cloud a voice: "This is my Son, my beloved. Listen to him." Suddenly looking around they no longer saw anyone with them — only Jesus.   *(Mark 9:2-8)*

SEEK AND FIND

IN THIS CLOUD OF UNKNOWING,
IN THIS CLOUD OF UNKNOWING

> . . . John of the Cross found silent music
> . . . Julian of Norwich discovered a courteous,
>   familiar God
> . . . Paul was taken into the heights of heaven
> . . . Augustine fell in love with the Lord
> . . . Teresa came home to an interior castle

IN THIS CLOUD OF UNKNOWING,
IN THIS CLOUD OF UNKNOWING

> . . . all clarity is turned into mystery
> . . . all self-righteousness yields to humility
> . . . all judgmentalism bows to compassion
> . . . all pride quakes before the divine presence
> . . . all arrogance falls before God's mountain

IN THIS CLOUD OF UNKNOWING,
IN THIS CLOUD OF UNKNOWING.

In this cloud of un - know - ing

PRAYER

Gracious Lord, our lives are filled with ambiguities. We long for sight but dwell so often in confusion and doubt. Help us to see; dispel the cloud of our ignorance. Do not hide your face from us but bring us into the presence of your joy and peace. May Jesus lead us through all clouds to you. *Amen.*

QUOTATIONS FROM FYODOR DOSTOEVSKY

He would again be as solitary as ever, and though he had great hopes, and great — too great — expectations from life, he could not have given any definite account of his hopes, his expectations, or even his desires.

———

You're a sensualist from your father, a crazy saint from your mother.

———

And there are some people who are better as foes than friends.

———

Because he was of the broad Karamazov character — that's just what I am leading up to — capable of combining the most incongruous contradictions, and capable of the greatest heights and of the greatest depths. Remember the brilliant remark made by a young observer who has seen the Karamazov family at close quarters — Mr. Rakitin: 'The sense of their own degradation is as essential to these reckless, unbridled natures as the sense of their lofty generosity.' And that's true, they need continually this unnatural mixture. Two extremes at the same moment, or they are miserable and dissatisfied and their existence is incomplete.[23]

LETTING GO

Most of us don't like twilight zones. When things are black or white at least we have clarity and know where we stand. Nebulosity has never been a favorite brand of ice cream — or inner disposition.

Some years ago I was thrown into a twilight zone. My reading skills were poor so I decided to take a speed reading course. The process began by breaking old habits. Initially this was difficult but with practice and persistence it was accomplished. One problem developed. Old patterns of reading poorly were broken; new ones had not yet fallen into place. I was in a no-man's land for several weeks. The twilight zone was pure gray.

Life's journey is crowded with ambiguities. They stand on every street corner and come knocking at every back door (sometimes so bold as to come in the door, uninvited). Whether we are falling in love, taking on a new job or experiencing the Lord in prayer, ambiguity filters its way in to break up our clarities. If it came alone we might be able to handle such a strange visitor. The difficulty is that it very often brings along two cousins: ambivalence and apprehension.

Yet there may well be an advantage hidden in the heart of this uninvited guest. Twilight zones and unclarity contain an opportunity to rethink our positions and lifestyles. Ambiguity can insert new factors into our decisions, challenge long-held assumptions, and even accuse us of crass assurance that should never have sprouted or been nurtured in the first place. Such job functions can promote human growth as well as the common good.

Was Tennessee Williams, the great playwright, correct when he wrote: "It is not the essential dignity but the essential ambiguity of man that I think needs to be stated"? State it he did in his plays; discover it we must in our own lives. On a clear day we can almost see forever—but such days are rare on the human journey. We desire the sign but are given many clouds of unknowing. These contain their own special clarity and truth.

Purification

MANTRA: **In the fire of God's love**

SOURCE: Catherine of Genoa's *Purgation and Purgatory*

Having come to the point of twenty-four carats,
gold cannot be purified any further;
and this is what happens to the soul
in the fire of God's love.
All of its imperfections are cast out like dross.
Once stripped of all its imperfections,
the soul rests in God, with no characteristics of its own,
since its purification
is the stripping away of the lower self in us.
Our being is then God.
Even if the soul were to remain in the fire,
still it would not consider that a suffering;
for those would be the flames of divine love,
of eternal life
such as the souls of the blessed enjoy.
Though this fire can be experienced in this life,
I do not believe that God allows such souls
to remain long on earth,
except to show His mighty works.[24]

PARALLEL REFERENCES

When the day of Pentecost came it found them gathered in one place. Suddenly from up in the sky there came a noise like a strong, driving wind which was heard all through the house where they were seated. Tongues as of fire appeared which parted and came to rest on each of them. All were filled with the Holy Spirit. They began to express themselves in foreign tongues and make bold proclamation as the Spirit prompted them.   *(Acts 2:1-4)*

Meanwhile Moses was tending the flock of his father-in-law Jethro, the priest of Midian. Leading the flock across the desert, he came to Horeb, the mountain of God. There an angel of the LORD appeared to him in fire flaming out of a bush. As he looked on, he was surprised to see that the bush, though on fire, was not consumed. So Moses decided, "I must go over to look at this remarkable sight, and see why the bush is not burned."

(Exodus 3:1-3)

FIRE AND ICE

IN THE FIRE OF GOD'S LOVE

the wetness of the log sizzles and crackles, turns black
and bursts into brilliant flames

IN THE FIRE OF GOD'S LOVE

the dross of our inhumanity evaporates into the night air

IN THE FIRE OF GOD'S LOVE

the glaciers that separate peoples and nations melt in a
golden convergence forming the river of life

IN THE FIRE OF GOD'S LOVE

the chilling westerly winds turn war into a caress and enkindle
the damp, cold earth

IN THE FIRE OF GOD'S LOVE

the golden piles of leaves are transformed into ashes
as a gift to the coming Spring

IN THE FIRE OF GOD'S LOVE

In the fire of God's love

PRAYER

God of fire and warmth, continue to melt the coldness of our
hearts, continue to illuminate the darkness of our world. May your
love burst into joy and enthusiasm as it touches our lives. May your
fire always be life-giving, calling us to conversion and zeal. Grant
this in the power of your Spirit. *Amen.*

QUOTATIONS FROM LOUIS DUPRÉ

Suffering is always unique to the person who suffers and separates him or her from all others. What mostly distinguishes the mystic from the ordinary person is his or her willingness to regard it, even in its most humiliating aspects, as a most individual vocation. The mystic is ready for the passive purgation because he or she has long learned to accept all suffering as a God-given chance to be purified.

Only in suffering does love prove its authenticity. Lovers of all ages have sought out hardship and denial, not merely as a token of love to the beloved, but to authenticate it for themselves. Suffering alone, if freely accepted, safeguards love against selfishness. For the creature at least, even for that creature who was personally united to God, loving means more than giving oneself—it means giving oneself up for the other.

To reach that primeval poverty, my poverty, which for Eckhart is also God's poverty, is the goal of the mystical journey. To attain it, the soul must abandon not only its possessions and its self-will, but also its creaturely identity and even its "God."[25]

THE SETTING SUN

Last evening as I was driving into the setting sun I discovered a valuable analogy. For just a short time the sun illuminated my windshield making visible the many tiny specks of dust which had been hardly discernible during the day. Now under the penetrating light of the sun they were rudely revealed.

Purity is the lesson that came home—purity being somehow linked with transparency—that what is seen is seen through. My windshield was not pure; the stain and grime of everyday life blocked the piercing brilliance of the sun. Imperfection renders vision incomplete. Reality becomes less tangible and whole. The analogy can be carried to every dimension of life—wherever transparency is blocked, purity is wanting.

As the rain gently yet forcefully cleanses the city streets so, too, does the fire of God's purifying love burn away all false gods. Our tendency is to avoid the flame at all costs. Thus much of life is spent trying to escape from that loving fire or in resisting what must come to pass. No one likes to suffer and purity will demand a price. Thus we are not surprised to realize that suffering becomes an imperative for most of us; it is not freely chosen in voluntary asceticism.

A log not thrown upon the fire remains a log. Once it's thrown on the fire, its transformation begins. The wetness is burned out; purification takes place. And then the glory—the log bursts into flames to scatter light and warmth. In this consummation the log's existence is ended—or has it just begun? The paradox remains—we live with mystery.

Driving into the western sun can be a lesson in purity. God's fire continues to burn—will we approach it in faith and wonder?

III.
Midnight Mantras
and the Poets

Loneliness

MANTRA: **Nothing except loneliness**

SOURCE: Poem by e. e. cummings

> no time ago
> or else in a life
> walking in the dark
> i met christ
>
> jesus) my heart
> flopped over
> and lay still
> while he passed(as
>
> close as i'm to you
> yes closer
> made of nothing
> except loneliness[26]

PARALLEL REFERENCES

Afterward he [Jesus] went out and saw a tax collector named Levi sitting at his customs post. He said to him, "Follow me." Leaving everything behind, Levi stood up and became his follower.

(Luke 5:27-28)

They came to Jericho next, and as he was leaving that place with his disciples and a sizable crowd, there was a blind beggar Bartimaeus ("son of Timaeus") sitting by the roadside. On hearing that it was

Jesus of Nazareth, he began to call out, "Jesus, Son of David, have pity on me!" Many people were scolding him to make him keep quiet, but he shouted all the louder, "Son of David, have pity on me!" Then, Jesus stopped and said, "Call him over." So they called the blind man over, telling him as they did so, "You have nothing to fear from him! Get up! He is calling you!" He threw aside his cloak, jumped up and came to Jesus. Jesus asked him, "What do you want me to do for you?" "Rabboni," the blind man said, "I want to see." Jesus said in reply, "Be on your way! Your faith has healed you." Immediately he received his sight and started to follow him up the road. *(Mark 10:46-52)*

DIVINE MELANCHOLY

NOTHING EXCEPT LONELINESS
NOTHING EXCEPT LONELINESS

      His eyes searched — no affection
      His hands touched — a cold response
      His words proclaimed — silence

NOTHING EXCEPT LONELINESS
NOTHING EXCEPT LONELINESS

      The roads crowded with loneliness
      The streets empty of meaning
      The mountain tops aloof from understanding

NOTHING EXCEPT LONELINESS
NOTHING EXCEPT LONELINESS

      Affection still given — without return
      Healing still offered — no gratitude
      Message still shared — despite deafness.

No - thing ex - cept lone - li - ness

PRAYER

Noble and gracious Lord, you walked the way of emptiness and poverty. No one can understand the sorrows of your heart. Grant us the privilege to share in your cup; grant us the strength to carry our cross. When you look back, may you find us close behind. *Amen.*

QUOTATIONS FROM LOREN EISELEY

But we, pale and alone and small in that immensity, hurled back the living stars. Somewhere far off, across bottomless abysses, I felt as though another world was flung more joyfully. I could have thrown in a frenzy of joy, but I set my shoulders and cast, as the thrower in the rainbow cast, slowly, deliberately, and well. The task was not to be assumed lightly, for it was men as well as starfish that we sought to save. For a moment, we cast on an infinite beach together beside an unknown hurler of suns. It was, unsought, the destiny of my kind since the rituals of the ice age hunters, when life in the Northern Hemisphere had come close to vanishing. We had lost our way, I thought, but we had kept, some of us, the memory of the perfect circle of compassion from life to death and back again to life—the completion of the rainbow of existence. Even the hunters in the snow, making obeisance to the souls of the hunted, had known the cycle. The legend had come down and lingered that he who gained the gratitude of animals gained help in need from the dark wood.

———

Lastly, we inhabit a spiritual twilight on this planet. It is perhaps the most poignant of all the deprivations to which man has been exposed by nature. I have said *deprivation*, but perhaps I should, rather, maintain that this feeling of loss is an unrealized anticipation. We imagine we are day creatures, but we grope in a lawless and smoky realm toward an exit that eludes us. We appear to know instinctively that such an exit exists.

———

Solitude may strike self-conscious man as an affliction, but his march is away from his origins, and even his art is increasingly abstract and self-centered. From the solitude of the wood he has passed to the more dreadful solitude of the heart.[27]

THE LONE OAK

The northern part of Wisconsin has magnificent forests and farmlands. Recently I saw a field being cleared of timber and prepared for cultivation. Interestingly, a large, single oak tree was left to stand in the center of the field, all of its companions swept away by chainsaws and bulldozers.

If that tree could have expressed its feelings about loneliness, we might have heard it say: "Oh, woe is me—divorced from my friends, buffeted by fierce winds in this open field, no one to talk to in the evenings—what has gone wrong?" Now we know oak trees aren't really lonely, but we humans, unfortunately, know the feeling all too well.

Loneliness comes at strange times in our lives: at the center of a wedding reception, upon waking at 3:00 A.M. to some strange noise, during a telephone conversation with a supposed friend, at the apex of prayer and worship. Though some might claim to be exempt from loneliness, I think the boast is slightly exaggerated. The human condition necessarily embraces some moments and even seasons of raw loneliness, as biting as any winter wind. The tragedy in human life is that sometimes loneliness comes and never leaves—an unwelcome guest indeed.

Simone Weil, a philosophical and spiritual writer of great depth, once expressed the desire to experience both affliction and joy in all their purity: affliction without any joy, joy without any affliction. A dangerous desire. To experience loneliness in its pure essence is to taste the edge of hell. Some endure that loneliness over a long period of time. If there is no end to it, one's psychological and spiritual life is endangered. Nothing except loneliness is a little too much—much too much.

Failure

MANTRA: **Best-laid schemes o' mice an' men**

SOURCE: Robert Burns' "To a Mouse on Turning Her Up In
Her Nest with the Plough, November, 1785"

> The best-laid schemes o' mice an' men
>   Gang aft agley,
> An' lea'e us naught but grief an' pain,
>   For promis'd joy!
>
> Still thou are blest, compared wi' me!
> The present only toucheth thee:
> But och! I backward cast my e'e,
>   On prospects drear!
> An' forward, tho' I canna see,
>   I guess an' fear![28]

PARALLEL REFERENCES

When Isaac was so old that his eyesight had failed him, he called his
older son Esau and said to him, "Son!" "Yes, father!" he replied.
Isaac then said, "As you can see, I am so old that I may now die at
any time. Take your gear, therefore — your quiver and bow — and
go out into the country to hunt some game for me. With your catch
prepare an appetizing dish for me, such as I like, and bring it to me
to eat, so that I may give you my special blessing before I die."
(Genesis 27:1-4)

The feast of Unleavened Bread known as the Passover was drawing
near, and the high priests and scribes began to look for some way to

dispose of him; but they were afraid of the people. Then Satan took possession of Judas, the one called Iscariot, a member of the Twelve. He went off to confer with the chief priests and officers about a way to hand him over to them. They were delighted, and agreed to give him money. He accepted, then kept looking for an opportunity to hand him over without creating a disturbance.

(Luke 22:1-6)

Best - laid schemes o' mice an' men

IF AT FIRST . . .

BEST-LAID SCHEMES O' MICE AN' MEN
BEST-LAID SCHEMES O' MICE AN' MEN

> Broken dreams
>> — the tower of Babel lost in the confusion of tongues
>> — gold in dem dar hills . . . only dust
>> — rainbow's end never found
>> — the surgeon's knife that cut too deep
>> — the dissertation delivered stillborn

BEST-LAID SCHEMES O' MICE AN' MEN
BEST-LAID SCHEMES O' MICE AN' MEN

> Broken relationships
>> — the marriage smashed on the rocks of discontent
>> — prayer turned sour by infidelity
>> — the serpent's tooth . . . an ungrateful child
>> — the heart of a friend infected by envy
>> — international "peace" founded on greed

BEST-LAID SCHEMES O' MICE AN' MEN
BEST-LAID SCHEMES O' MICE AN' MEN

Best - laid schemes o' mice an' men

PRAYER

God, your divine plan of love and forgiveness comes to us daily in the unfolding of history. Our own plans so often fail because they are not in accord with your providence. Help us to know your blueprint and to base our plans on your word. Thus we will bring your peace and joy to all we meet. May your best-laid plans always find a home in our hearts. *Amen.*

QUOTATIONS FROM LOREN EISELEY

"But I *do* love the world," I whispered to a waiting presence in the empty room. "I love its small ones, the things beaten in the strangling surf, the bird, singing, which flies and falls and is not seen again." I choked and said, with the torn eye still upon me, "I love the lost ones, the failures of the world."

———

"The conviction of wisdom," wrote Montaigne in the sixteenth century, "is the plague of man." Century after century, humanity studies itself in the mirror of fashion, and ever the mirror gives back distortions, which for the moment impose themselves upon man's real image. In one period we believe ourselves governed by immutable laws; in the next, by chance. In one period angels hover over our birth; in the following time we are planetary waifs, the product of a meaningless and ever altering chemistry. We exchange halos in one era for fangs in another. Our religious and philosophical conceptions change so rapidly that the theological and moral exhortations of one decade become the wastepaper of the next epoch. The ideas for which millions yielded up their lives produce only bored yawns in a later generation.

———

Perhaps it is always the destined role of the compassionate to be strangers among men. To fail and pass, to fail and come again. For the seed of man is thistledown, and a puff of breath may govern it, or a word from a poet torment it into greatness. There are few among us who can notice the passage of a moth's wing across an opera tent at midnight and ask ourselves, "Whose is the real play?"[29]

WILLY LOMAN

Willy Loman was a failure — on two counts. He failed as a father; he failed in being able to support his family by means of the business world. Thus Arthur Miller, creator of Willy Loman, entitles his play *The Death of a Salesman*. As the play so aptly shows,

Willy Loman died long before he reached the grave. In that lay his tragedy.

Failure has to do with expectations. Goals are set at many levels: to attain a certain income during the next year, to read certain books within a given time frame, to lose twenty pounds in a fitness program, to spend more time with the children, to devote a half hour a day to prayer. When these go unrealized, for whatever reason, there is a sense of failure, especially when a reasonable amount of effort has been expended. In some instances guilt and shame enter in to aggravate the situation. One day there is the recognition that a pattern of failure has been established. Willy Loman lived in this land.

A warning is necessary: by what standard are we to judge success or failure on the human journey? From the human vantage point, which tends to see success primarily in material acquisitions and various professional achievements (Ph.D., etc.), we are simply buying into our cultural and societal value system. From the biblical point of view, success and/or failure is grounded in the criteria of love and fidelity to relationships. Only the life that is truly void of love, either the giving or receiving of it, falls into the category of failure. From this perspective was Willy Loman really a failure?

Schemes and plans are important. Yet in laying them out we must be most discerning as to what they really are and how they are to be achieved. The experience of failure is very relative when judged from different perspectives.

Pain

MANTRA: **The exact time of the knife**

SOURCE: Edward Seifert's "Pain"

You will never be as alone as now
In the sudden flare and stab of it
There in your side where the ribs sit.
You live in the strictest privacy
You will ever be knowing.
No hand can soothe, no mind can reach
The darkened cage where you toss.
The stabs are staggered. You can never know
The exact time of the knife.
You have learned too well that your pain
Is yours, inalienably yours.
This evil you have learned to claim
As yours, undeniably yours,
Even as a harassed father must claim
His basest child and most hideous.[30]

PARALLEL REFERENCES

Simon Peter, in company with another disciple, kept following
Jesus closely. This disciple, who was known to the high priest,
stayed with Jesus as far as the high priest's courtyard, while Peter
was left standing at the gate. The disciple known to the high priest
came out and spoke to the woman at the gate, and then brought
Peter in. This servant girl who kept the gate said to Peter, "Are you
not one of this man's followers?" "Not I," he replied.

(John 18:15-17)

The king [David] was shaken, and went up to the room over the city gate to weep. He said as he wept, "My son, Absalom! My son, my son Absalom! If only I had died instead of you, Absalom, my son, my son!" *(2 Samuel 19:1)*

STEEL BLADE

THE EXACT TIME OF THE KNIFE
THE EXACT TIME OF THE KNIFE

> December 7, 1941 . . . planes over Pearl Harbor
> August 6, 1945 . . . a mushroom cloud
> November 22, 1963 . . . the death of a president
> September 1, 1983 . . . Korean Airliner KAL 007 shot
>   down
> October 23, 1983 . . . 264 marines killed while sleeping

THE EXACT TIME OF THE KNIFE
THE EXACT TIME OF THE KNIFE . . .

> the floods of spring . . . all carried away in wild torrents
> the storms of summer . . . when conflicts abound
> the hurricanes of autumn . . . with nothing to hang on to
> the blizzards of winter . . . freezing the human heart and
>   its loves
> the knell of day . . . when all is decided

THE EXACT TIME OF THE KNIFE
THE EXACT TIME OF THE KNIFE.

The ex - act time of the knife

PRAYER

Your word is a two-edged sword, O Lord. You come to bring us life but also to cut away all that is deadly and destructive. We do not know the exact time or hour of your visitation. Come with your mercy and compassion but do come and do not leave us in darkness. Grant this through Jesus, the divine and loving surgeon. *Amen.*

QUOTATIONS FROM WILLIAM SHAKESPEARE

Infirmity doth still neglect all office
Whereto our health is bound; we are not ourselves
When nature, being oppress'd, commands the mind
To suffer with the body.

———

Thou think'st 'tis much that this contentious storm
Invades us to the skin. So 'tis to thee,
But where the greater malady is fix'd,
The lesser is scarce felt. Thou'dst shun a bear,
But if thy flight lay toward the roaring sea,
Thou'dst meet the bear in' th' mouth. When the mind's free,
The body's delicate. The tempest in my mind
Doth from my senses take all feeling else
Save what beats there.

———

When we our betters see bearing our woes,
We scarcely think our miseries our foes.
Who alone suffers suffers most i' th' mind,
Leaving free things and happy shows behind.[31]

THE SURGEON'S TABLE

My father's medical office was attached to our family home. As my
doctor-father went off to the hospital in the early morning, I would
frequently wander into his office attracted by the strange smells
and sights, intrigued by this marvelous world of bandages and pills.
Always I would ponder the surgical knives resting near a small
sterilizing unit. My wonder was also filled with fear, knowing that
these shining blades bit deeply into human flesh.

My father was a gentle man. How could he cut open a human
body? From a child's perspective it seemed so cruel. The paradox
settled uneasily in my soul: health brought about by pain. Was this
some cruel and perplexing joke? The dentist extracting the deeply
rooted tooth, the surgeon's incision finding the infection, the

teacher's rod bringing painful but necessary discipline. Some people are unable to wield the knife. Others can, and in so doing they foster life.

Over the years my amazement has grown as I view the wide variety of knives that we use on our journey: indeed, the physical knife of the surgeon, but also the psychological knives of words spoken or unspoken; the spiritual knives of asceticism and mortification; the societal knives of imprisonment and isolation. Though we do not know the exact time when the blade will enter our own experience, we know beyond doubt that it will come. Infection is too universal to pass us by. Though the pain will be there, the lessons of life teach us that such suffering is necessary for the sake of life. Without the blade the infection remains to bring its own death.

Our identity is that of both surgeon and patient. Sometimes we wield the knife, sometimes we receive it. Both must be accompanied by love and courage.

Death

MANTRA: **The undiscover'd country**

SOURCE: Shakespeare's *Hamlet*

To be, or not to be, that is the question:
Whether 'tis nobler in the mind to suffer
The slings and arrows of outrageous fortune,
Or to take arms against a sea of troubles,
And by opposing end them. To die, to sleep—
No more—and by a sleep to say we end
The heart-ache and the thousand natural shocks
That flesh is heir to. 'Tis a consummation
Devoutly to be wish'd. To die, to sleep;
To sleep, perchance to dream. Ay, there's the rub,
For in that sleep of death what dreams may come
When we have shuffled off this mortal coil,
Must give us pause. There's the respect
That makes calamity of so long life.
For who would bear the whips and scorns of time,
Th' oppressor's wrong, the proud man's contumely,
The pangs of despis'd love, the law's delay,
The insolence of office, and the spurns
That patient merit of th' unworthy takes,
When he himself might his quietus make
With a bare bodkin? Who would fardels bear,
To grunt and sweat under a weary life,
But that the dread of something after death,
The undiscover'd country from whose bourn
No traveler returns, puzzles the will,
And makes us rather bear those ills we have
Than fly to others that we know not of?[32]

It was a cave with a stone laid across it. "Take away the stone," Jesus directed. Martha, the dead man's sister, said to him, "Lord, it has been four days now; surely there will be a stench!" Jesus replied, "Did I not assure you that if you believed you would see the glory of God displayed?" They then took away the stone and Jesus looked upward and said:

> "Father, I thank you for having heard me.
> I know that you always hear me
> but I have said this for the sake of the crowd,
> that they may believe that you sent me."

Having said this he called loudly, "Lazarus, come out!" The dead man came out, bound hand and foot with linen strips, his face wrapped in a cloth. "Untie him," Jesus told them, "and let him go free."   *(John 11:38-44)*

Before Jesus had finished speaking to them, a synagogue leader came up, did him reverence, and said: "My daughter has just died. Please come and lay your hand on her and she will come back to life." Jesus stood up and followed him, and his disciples did the same . . . . When Jesus arrived at the synagogue leader's house and saw the flute players and the crowd who were making a din, he said, "Leave, all of you! The little girl is not dead. She is asleep." At this they began to ridicule him. When the crowd had been put out he entered and took her by the hand, and the little girl got up. News of this circulated throughout the district. *(Matthew 9:18-19, 23-26)*

INFERNO REVISITED

THE UNDISCOVER'D COUNTRY,
THE UNDISCOVER'D COUNTRY

> . . . what games are played on your city streets?
> . . . what books populate your libraries?
> . . . why are your secrets so well kept?
> . . . are any passports ever granted?
> . . . do you have seasons?

THE UNDISCOVER'D COUNTRY,
THE UNDISCOVER'D COUNTRY

> . . . what roads and paths do your people travel?
> . . . do birds still sing their songs in your land?
> . . . who are your heroes and models?
> . . . is your kingdom democratic?
> . . . what resides beyond your black hole?

THE UNDISCOVER'D COUNTRY,
THE UNDISCOVER'D COUNTRY.

The un - dis - cov - er ed coun - try

PRAYER

Lord, we cannot see beyond the limitations of time and space. We do not know the land of death nor the world of resurrection. Help us to live well now so that when we gain entrance into this undiscover'd country we may bring gifts of peace and joy. Calm our anxieties about the journey, still our fears with your promised presence. Grant those in this land fullness of life. We ask this in the name of your Son Jesus. *Amen.*

QUOTATIONS FROM ERNEST BECKER

. . . death is man's peculiar and greatest anxiety.

———

The knowledge of death is reflective and conceptual, and animals are spared it. They live and they disappear with the same thoughtlessness: a few minutes of fear, a few seconds of anguish, and it is over. But to live a whole lifetime with the fate of death haunting one's dreams and even the most sun-filled days—that's something else.

———

Kierkegaard had his own formula for what it means to be a man. He put it forth in those superb pages wherein he describes what he calls "the knight of faith." This figure is the man who lives in faith, who has given over the meaning of life to his Creator, and who lives centered on the energies of his Maker. He accepts whatever happens in this visible dimension without complaint, lives his life as a duty, faces his death without a qualm. No pettiness is so petty that it threatens his meanings; no task is too frightening to be beyond his courage. He is fully in the world on its terms and wholly beyond the world in his trust in the invisible dimension. It is very much the old Pietistic ideal that was lived by Kant's parents. The great strength of such an ideal is that it allows one to be open, generous, courageous, to touch others' lives and enrich them and open them in turn. As the knight of faith has no fear-of-life-and-death trip to lay onto others, he does not cause them to shrink back upon themselves, he does not coerce or manipulate them. The knight of faith, then, represents what we might call an ideal of mental health, the continuing openness of life out of the death throes of dread.[33]

THE UNEXPECTED GUEST

They found his body on the floor. An hour before, he had sat at table, enjoying food and laughter, then had gone for a walk in the cool evening. Suddenly, back in his room, my friend was called to the undiscover'd country – the land of death. When I arrived his hands were cold, his mouth locked open, his body contorted from the last moment of pain.

What lies behind the veil of death? Here is the body but where is the spirit? What happens when time ends and eternity begins? Who is there on the other side to greet him? A hundred more questions rushed torrent-like through the riverbed of my mind.

No longer would we share meals or stories together, no longer take trips to visit autumn or welcome spring, no longer share the short note or quick phone call. Death brought all that to a sharp end. Death has no mercy on the living.

My friend found departures hard – the ending of a phone conversation would be abrupt, the parting at the end of the day would be swift. Why not die the way one lives? A fast, quick exit? Perhaps the quickness removes embarrassment. But his death came too swiftly. Not even time for a quick goodbye.

A friend dies but friendship is not ended. Its roots are in eternity. Though conversation and trips are temporal adventures, something more lasting lies at the center. Death cannot sever that bond; death has no power over love.

The river has been crossed to that undiscover'd country. No vision can make out the contours of the land but faith tells us it does exist. Here theory is of no use. Only those who get into the boat and make the journey themselves come into knowledge. My friend now knows – and he awaits my arrival.

Mutability

MANTRA: **Clouds that veil the midnight moon**

SOURCE: Percy Bysshe Shelley's "Mutability"

We are as clouds that veil the midnight moon;
  How restlessly they speed, and gleam, and quiver,
Streaking the darkness radiantly! — yet soon
  Night closes round, and they are lost forever:

Or like forgotten lyres, whose dissonant strings
  Give various response to each varying blast,
To whose frail frame no second motion brings
  One mood or modulation like the last.

We rest. — A dream has power to poison sleep;
  We rise. — One wandering thought pollutes the day;
We feel, conceive or reason, laugh or weep;
  Embrace fond woe, or cast our cares away:

It is the same! — For, be it joy or sorrow,
  The path of its departure still is free:
Man's yesterday may ne'er be like his morrow;
  Nought may endure but Mutability.[34]

PARALLEL REFERENCES

What has been, that will be; what has been done, that will be done.
Nothing is new under the sun. Even the thing of which we say,
"See, this is new!" has already existed in the ages that preceded us.

There is no remembrance of the men of old; nor of those to come will there be any remembrance among those who come after them.
(Ecclesiastes 1:9-11)

"Do not live in fear, little flock. It has pleased your Father to give you the kingdom. Sell what you have and give alms. Get purses for yourselves that do not wear out, a never-failing treasure with the Lord which no thief comes near nor any moth destroys. Wherever your treasure lies, there your heart will be." *(Luke 12:32-34)*

MIDNIGHT MOON

CLOUDS THAT VEIL THE MIDNIGHT MOON
CLOUDS THAT VEIL THE MIDNIGHT MOON

     also . . .
        veil my heart from deep experience
        obscure the truth of love and pain
        block the forces of justice and freedom
        separate one people from another
        lance the light from darkness

CLOUDS THAT VEIL THE MIDNIGHT MOON
CLOUDS THAT VEIL THE MIDNIGHT MOON

     remind us . . .
        of the shifting sands of seasons and times
        of the transitory nature of spring dandelions
        of the struggle for security and clarity
        of things too mysterious to hold in one's hand

CLOUDS THAT VEIL THE MIDNIGHT MOON
CLOUDS THAT VEIL THE MIDNIGHT MOON.

Clouds that veil the mid - night moon

PRAYER

Gracious and loving God, Lord of earth and sky, you teach us
many lessons in the events of nature. As the clouds obscure the
midnight moon we puzzle over the sudden loss of light, the swift
approach of darkness. As the clouds block the sun, we sometimes
lose our way and doubt many things. Do not remain behind the
clouds but come to us in clarity and joy. May the changeableness of
life not cause us to weaken or to become discouraged. Be our light
and our salvation. *Amen.*

QUOTATIONS FROM HERMAN MELVILLE

But Queequeg, do you see, was a creature in the transition stage — neither caterpillar nor butterfly.

———

There is no steady unretracing progress in this life; we do not advance through fixed gradations, and at the last one pause: — through infancy's unconscious spell, boyhood's thoughtless faith, adolescence' doubt (the common doom), then scepticism, then disbelief, resting at last in manhood's pondering repose of If. But once gone through, we trace the round again; and are infants, boys, and men, and Ifs eternally.

———

I've . . . changed my flesh since that time, why not my mind?

———

"What is it, what nameless, inscrutable, unearthly thing is it; what cozening, hidden lord and master, and cruel, remorseless emperor commands me; that against all natural lovings and longings, I so keep pushing, and crowding, and jamming myself on all the time; recklessly making me ready to do what in my own proper, natural heart, I durst not so much as dare? Is Ahab, Ahab? Is it I, God, or who, that lifts this arm?[35]

COUNT DRACULA

I woke up screaming. In an instant my mother was at my bedside trying to quiet my fears. I explained to her, in my four-year-old voice, that I had just seen Count Dracula outside my window and that he was trying to get in. We talked for some time before sleep once again descended upon me.

When the clouds veil the moon and sun, be it midnight or noon, fears begin to race through the fragile human heart. The phobias are many — those malignant diseases of the what-if's — and they come upon us in all seasons but especially in darkness and in times of radical change. In adulthood, the words of a mother are too distant to squelch the terrors of the night; the thoughts of philosophers, too abstract and esoteric to bring relief; the vision of faith, too blurred by the immediacy of doubt. The human condition throws us into terror at the mystery of death, into terror at the overwhelmingness of life. People who die well and live intensely are not numerous.

Is there anything on this life's journey that is immutable? All the great people have in some way answered yes and have tried to describe that immutable quality of life in a variety of ways, but ultimately the word expressed is *love.* The mother's voice calming a night fear, the gentle reassurance from a long distant friend, the welling up of affection in the human heart—each of these has a note of eternity attached to it. Though they appear transitory, they are lasting, each in its own way. Not even death can take them away.

Some years ago there was a popular song entitled "Both Sides Now." The lyrics spoke of clouds as ice cream castles in the air and also as blocking the sun. Clouds, like all of life, have an ambivalent character. Much depends upon our interpretation; much depends upon our vision of life.

Meaninglessness

MANTRA: **What had I on earth to do?**

SOURCE: Robert Browning's "Epilogue to 'Asolando'"

At the midnight in the silence of the sleep-time,
    When you set your fancies free,
Will they pass to where — by death, fools think, imprisoned —
Low he lies who once so loved you, whom you loved so,
                    — Pity me?
Oh to love so, be so loved, yet so mistaken!
    What had I on earth to do
With the slothful, with the mawkish, the unmanly?
Like the aimless, helpless, hopeless, did I drivel
                    — Being — who?
One who never turned his back but marched breast forward,
    Never doubted clouds would break,
Never dreamed, though right were worsted, wrong would triumph,
Held we fall to rise, are baffled to fight better,
                    Sleep to wake.
No, at noonday in the bustle of man's work-time
    Greet the unseen with a cheer!
Bid him forward, breast and back as either should be,
"Strive and thrive!" cry "Speed — fight on, fare ever
                    There as here!"[36]

PARALLEL REFERENCES

Vanity of vanities, says Qoheleth, vanity of vanities!
    All things are vanity!

What profit has man from all the labor which he toils at under the
   sun?
One generation passes and another comes, but the world forever
   stays.
The sun rises and the sun goes down; then it presses on to the place
   where it rises.
Blowing now toward the south, then toward the north,
   the wind turns again and again, resuming its rounds.
All rivers go to the sea, yet never does the sea become full.
To the place where they go, the rivers keep on going.
All speech is labored; there is nothing man can say.
The eye is not satisfied with seeing nor is the ear filled with hearing.

(Ecclesiastes 1:2-8)

The message of the cross is complete absurdity to those who are headed for ruin, but to us who are experiencing salvation it is the power of God. Scripture says, "I will destroy the wisdom of the wise, and thwart the cleverness of the clever." Where is the wise man to be found? Where the scribe? Where is the master of worldly argument? Has not God turned the wisdom of this world into folly? Since in God's wisdom the world did not come to know him through "wisdom," it pleased God to save those who believe through the absurdity of the preaching of the gospel. Yes, Jews demand "signs" and Greeks look for "wisdom," but we preach Christ crucified — a stumbling block to Jews, and an absurdity to Gentiles; but to those who are called, Jews and Greeks alike, Christ the power of God and the wisdom of God. For God's folly is wiser than men, and his weakness more powerful than men.

(1 Corinthians 1:18-25)

TO DO OR NOT TO DO

WHAT HAD I ON EARTH TO DO?
WHAT HAD I ON EARTH TO DO?

mow the endlessly growing lawn　? ? ?

? ? ?

speak and write words soon to be forgotten　? ? ?
build a home that time will crumble　? ? ?
raise a family that will ultimately die　? ? ?

? ? ?

paint a sunset that sunlight fades　? ? ?

WHAT HAD I ON EARTH TO DO?
WHAT HAD I ON EARTH TO DO?

bring order into the extravagance of nature　! ! !

! ! !

speak a word that heals and enlivens   !!!
provide shelter on a cold planet   !!!
participate in creation and human love   !!!

!!!

be captured by beauty and respond with
reverence   !!!

WHAT HAD I ON EARTH TO DO?
WHAT HAD I ON EARTH TO DO?

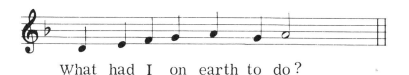

What had I on earth to do?

PRAYER

Lord, we struggle on our pilgrimage. Our human condition is filled
with the finite and transitory. We long for the eternal and forever.
Help us to believe that there is more than what we see; help us to
hope for what can be. Make our lives an act of love and fill them
with meaning and purpose. *Amen.*

QUOTATIONS FROM ROBERT STONE

A chill touched his inward loneliness. He was, he knew at that moment, really without beliefs, without hope—either for himself or
for the world. Almost without friends, certainly without allies.
Alone.

———

'What are you worth? Explain yourself."
"Everybody's worth something," Pablo said, "I mean—everybody's

life got some meaning to it. You know—there's a reason for people."

"No kidding? A reason for you? What is it?"

"I don't know," Pablo confessed, "I ain't found out yet. But I know there is one."

He was alone and lost, in outer darkness without friend or faction. It was a frightening place—the point he had been working toward since the day he had come south. It was his natural, self-appointed place.[37]

A SUMMER IMPERATIVE

At our Friday noon meal the imperative was given: "It's Friday and time to mow the lawn." Although this command infringed upon my baseball time, my resistance was deeper than mere lack of play. My twelve-year-old heart felt a sense of futility sweep over it as I pushed the lawn mower through the backyard. Why do this? Seven days from now the grass will be once again in need of trimming. The foolishness and meaninglessness of the task weighed heavily upon my young spirit.

The farmer plowing his field, the heart surgeon scrubbing for surgery, the teacher preparing a lesson, the preacher writing out the sermon, the tour guide describing the architecture of the pyramid, the philosopher completing a lengthy manuscript—all these people involved in some task. But that doing demands a meaning and a motive. Surely each of them has days if not weeks in which the purpose of the work is questioned. Is there any ultimate value to this particular endeavor? Is there anything which is eternal?

The poet Jessica Powers addresses the issue of our eternal quest to discover reasons for our seemingly meaningless existence:

> Obscurity becomes the final peace.
> The hidden then are the elect, the free.
> They leave our garish noon and find their peace
> in evening's gift of anonymity.

Lost not in loneness but in multitude
they serve unseen, without the noise of name.
Should you disdain them, ponder for your good:
it was in this way that the angels came.[38]

I no longer mow lawns but I am glad that young people still do. We each have a task to perform—the task of bringing order, justice, peace, and freedom into our world.

Nothingness

MANTRA: **Neither joy, nor love, nor light**

SOURCE: Matthew Arnold's "Dover Beach"

The sea is calm tonight.
The tide is full, the moon lies fair
Upon the straits; — on the French coast the light
Gleams and is gone; the cliffs of England stand,
Glimmering and vast, out in the tranquil bay.
Come to the window, sweet is the night-air!

Only, from the long line of spray
Where the sea meets the moon-blanched land,
Listen! you hear the grating roar
Of pebbles which the waves draw back, and fling,
At their return, up the high strand,
Begin, and cease, and then again begin,
With tremulous cadence slow, and bring
The eternal note of sadness in.

Sophocles long ago
Heard it on the Aegean, and it brought
Into his mind the turbid ebb and flow
Of human misery; we
Find also in the sound a thought,
Hearing it by this distant northern sea.

The Sea of Faith
Was once, too, at the full and round earth's shore
Lay like the folds of a bright girdle furled.

But now I only hear
Its melancholy, long, withdrawing roar,
Retreating, to the breath
Of the night-wind, down the vast edges drear
And naked shingles of the world.

Ah, love, let us be true
To one another! for the world, which seems
To lie before us like a land of dreams,
So various, so beautiful, so new,
Hath really neither joy, nor love, nor light,
Nor certitude, nor peace, nor help for pain;
And we are here as on a darkling plain
Swept with confused alarms of struggle and flight,
Where ignorant armies clash by night.[39]

PARALLEL REFERENCES

My eyes have grown dim through affliction;
    daily I call upon you, O LORD;
    to you I stretch out my hands.
Will you work wonders for the dead?
    Will the shades arise to give you thanks?
Do they declare your kindness in the grave,
    your faithfulness among those who have perished?
Are your wonders made known in the darkness,
    or your justice in the land of oblivion?   *(Psalm 88:10-13)*

Job spoke out and said:
    Perish the day on which I was born,
        the night when they said, "The child is a boy!"
    May that day be darkness:
        let not God above call for it, nor light shine upon it!
                                    (Job 3:2-4)

NIHIL

NEITHER JOY, NOR LOVE, NOR LIGHT,
NEITHER JOY, NOR LOVE, NOR LIGHT —

    No word of affirmation though the job was well done
    No letter of acceptance though the manuscript was flawless
      and profound
    No experience of hope though the sun shone and the birds
      sang
    No human touch though the crowd was great, the people
      many
    No understanding though the words were simple, the stories
      strong

NEITHER JOY, NOR LOVE, NOR LIGHT,
NEITHER JOY, NOR LOVE, NOR LIGHT —

    No fruit on the tree though the roots were well tended
    No tear in the eyes though the friend had died

No frown of dismay though injustice was obvious
No smile of affection though the gift was tender and holy

NEITHER JOY, NOR LOVE, NOR LIGHT,
NEITHER JOY, NOR LOVE, NOR LIGHT —

No hospitality though the guest had been cordially invited
No consolation though the gifts were many
No listening love though the pain was deep
No tender embrace though the isolation could be felt
No holy fear though the dangers were many

NEITHER JOY, NOR LOVE, NOR LIGHT,
NEITHER JOY, NOR LOVE, NOR LIGHT.

Nei - ther joy, nor love, nor light

PRAYER

Lord, in the seasons of nothingness, do not let us remain empty for
long. Fill us not with things but with your presence. Bring us the
joy of knowing that you are faithful and near. May our
nothingness be a means of disposing our hearts to embrace yourself
and your creation. Grant this in your gracious time. *Amen.*

QUOTATIONS FROM SAINT JOHN OF THE CROSS

This is how we recognize the person who truly loves God; if he is
content with nothing less than God. But what am I saying, if he is
content? Even if he possesses everything, he will not be content; in
fact the more he has, the less satisfied he will be. Satisfaction of
heart is not found in the possession of things, but in being stripped
of them all and in poverty of spirit. Since perfection consists in this
poverty of spirit, in which God is possessed by a very intimate and

special grace, the soul, having attained it, lives in this life with some satisfaction, although not complete.

———

It is noteworthy that God is very ready to comfort and satisfy the soul in her needs and afflictions when she neither has nor desires consolation and satisfaction outside of Him. The soul possessing nothing that might withhold her from God cannot remain long without a visit from the Beloved.

———

. . . God does not fit in an occupied heart.

———

Even though he was manifestly rich, he says he was poor because his will was not fixed on riches; and he thereby lived as though really poor. On the other hand, had he been actually poor, without his will being so, there would have been no true poverty, because the appetite of his soul would have been rich and full.[40]

CORDELIA: NOTHING OR ALL

In Shakespeare's *King Lear* there is an exchange between the king and his daughter Cordelia. The king will divide his kingdom among his three daughters in proportion to their love for him. Regan and Goneril, the first two daughters, protest their love profusely. Cordelia has a different response:

> Lear: Speak.
> Cordelia: Nothing, my lord.
> Lear: Nothing?
> Cordelia: Nothing.
> Lear: Nothing will come of nothing. Speak again.
> Cordelia: Unhappy that I am, I cannot heave
>   My heart into my mouth. I love your Majesty
>   According to my bond, no more nor less.[41]

Cordelia's "nothing" contains an integrity and honesty not possessed by her sisters. They were not concerned about the kingdom nor their father — only with gain and power. They would profess anything to gain it, using whatever means to obtain their end. Ultimately, all would come to nothing for them whereas Cordelia's original nothing would become everything.

There are few models of such self-abnegation in our contemporary world. The nothingness entailed in a basic poverty of life is shunned. Immediate gratification has become a way of life and in making this choice, personal authenticity and freedom is lost. Nothingness is considered a disease no less malignant than cancer. Whoever contracts it has a short time to live.

Yet there is in nothingness a reverse fullness. By detachment from all things we open up the possibility of encounter and union with all things. For some, that union will be achieved by passing through particular things into the mystery of God; for others, even finite reality must be foregone if that is the road given. The path of nothingness is not to be walked by all; yet, for that very reason, it must not be denigrated. Nothingness is a high road traveled by few; it is the most direct route home.

Cordelia teaches us a lesson. Nothing is better than any portion of reality which is lie. It was a lesson she lived and died.

Forgotten

MANTRA: **And blank oblivion comes**

SOURCE: From Thomas Hardy's 'The To-Be-Forgotten'

I

I heard a small sad sound,
And stood awhile among the tombs around:
'Wherefore, old friends,' said I, 'are you distrest,
Now, screened from life's unrest?'

II

'O not at being here;
But that our future second death is near;
When, with the living, memory of us numbs,
And blank oblivion comes!

III

'These, our sped ancestry,
Lie here embraced by deeper death than we;
Nor shape nor thought of theirs can you descry
With keenest backward eye.

IV

'They count as quite forgot;
They are as men who have existed not;
theirs is a loss past loss of fitful breath;
It is the second death . . . '[42]

133

PARALLEL REFERENCES

My God, my God, why have you forsaken me,
    far from my prayer, from the words of my cry?
O my God, I cry out by day, and you answer not;
    by night and there is no relief for me. *(Psalm 22:2-3)*

Then, taking bread and giving thanks, he broke it and gave it to
them, saying: "This is my body to be given for you. Do this as a
remembrance of me." He did the same with the cup after eating,
saying as he did so: "This cup is the new covenant in my blood,
which will be shed for you."   *(Luke 22:19-20)*

EARLY SENILITY

AND BLANK OBLIVION CAME
AND BLANK OBLIVION CAME

> DURING the second refrain of the Tennessee Waltz
> WHEN the sun went to sleep in the west
> AS the creeping vines buried the tombstone
> AFTER the fourth glass of wine on an empty stomach
> WITH a cry of anguish and farewell

AND BLANK OBLIVION CAME
AND BLANK OBLIVION CAME

> AS Judas refused to look into the eyes of Jesus
> AS Socrates drank the poison hemlock
> AS Hamlet walked the midnight watch with his father's
>   ghost
> AS a Dallas bullet tore through the body of a president
> AS the anesthetist exercised his quieting skill

AND BLANK OBLIVION CAME
AND BLANK OBLIVION CAME

> WITH graciousness, removing every moment of pain
> WITH hostility, resentful of so many happy days
> WITH seductiveness, promising some false dreams
> WITH ambivalence, pulling the heart in many direc-
>   tions
> WITH puzzlement, throwing us once again into the
>   maze of life

AND BLANK OBLIVION CAME
AND BLANK OBLIVION CAME

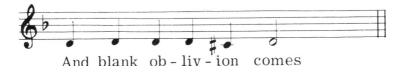

And blank ob - liv - ion comes

PRAYER

God of fidelity, do not forget us, your people. Grace us with a memory that recalls your abiding presence. Too forgetful are our hearts, too fickle our commitments. Instill within us the remembrance of your love and let that grace forever direct and govern our lives. *Amen.*

QUOTATIONS FROM JESSICA POWERS

The soul that cries to God out of the hot heart of contrition
is indisputably heard.
Here is the pact of love; it is triply signed with a sure eternal seal.
Though the whimpering call creeps out from the den of the coiled
    serpent
that hides from God and lies in wait for the Virgin's heel,
it stirs a sudden hastening out of heaven
to the place of the cry. God takes this piteous one at its urgent
    word.
He bundles it into His ship, with all its holdings,
and the island of sin is left behind, in distance blurred.
And He who redeems will use for the soul
the full extent of its cargo:
the songs, the memory's trivia, the sweet or acid tears,
the spoils or the debt of frightening arrears.
Ingenious to save, in the end His love will put to divine advantage
the wisdom (if wisdom could be the word) of the wasted years.

———

In the beginning, in the unbeginning
of endlessness and of eternity,
God saw this tree.
He saw these cedar branches bending low
under the full exhaustion of the snow.
And since He set no wind of day to rising,
this burden of beauty and this burden of cold,
(whether the wood breaks or the branches hold)
must be of His devising.

There is a cedar similarly decked
deep in the winter of my intellect
under the snow, the snow.
The scales of light its limitations tell.

I clasp this thought: from all eternity
God who is good looked down upon this tree
white in the weighted air,
and of another cedar reckoned well.
He knew how much each tree, each twig could bear.
He counted every snowflake as it fell.[43].

THE CHILD IN THE WOMB

Isaiah the prophet records his insight into the heart of a loving God. Even though a mother might be able to forget the child of her womb, it is impossible for God to forget his people. Such words contain a deep consolation. For, of all human needs, one of the deepest is to be remembered, one of the greatest pains is to be forgotten.

We humans war against forgetfulness: we take photographs to capture special celebrations; we exchange rings as reminders of our love and as a call to fidelity; we put our love letters in a special drawer lest the early movements of romanticism be washed to the sea. Time is fleeting. One event follows so quickly upon another. The stimuli of life overwhelm us and oblivion tends to eliminate the past. The battle to retain our memories records few victories.

In the corridors of old age the greatest fight is waged. As the arteries begin to harden, the memories are squeezed out or given no access to the heart. Gradually the glimmer in the eyes of the elderly is dulled and the memories of home and spouse and even faith become blurred and often disappear. This last poverty is perhaps the most painful of all. Ever so often a lucid day is gained when memories flood back with sudden surprise. Then just as suddenly they evaporate like the morning dew.

For two thousand years the Christian community has sung a constant refrain given to it by the Lord: "Do this in remembrance of me." Herein resides our hope — the celebration of that Eucharist of obedience and self-giving in Jesus. Even though oblivion may sweep over individuals within the community, obscuring the past and blurring the future, the community continues to carry the history of salvation within its heart. Blank oblivion will never win this battle.

Night

MANTRA: **One acquainted with the night**

SOURCE: Robert Frost's "Acquainted with the Night"

> I have been one acquainted with the night.
> I have walked out in rain—and back in rain.
> I have outwalked the furthest city light.
>
> I have looked down the saddest city lane.
> I have passed by the watchman on his beat
> And dropped my eyes, unwilling to explain.
>
> I have stood still and stopped the sound of feet
> When far away an interrupted cry
> Came over houses from another street,
>
> But not to call me back or say good-by;
> And further still at an unearthly height,
> One luminary clock against the sky
>
> Proclaimed the time was neither wrong nor right.
> I have been one acquainted with the night.[44]

PARALLEL REFERENCES

A certain Pharisee named Nicodemus, a member of the Jewish Sanhedrin, came to him at night. "Rabbi," he said, "we know you are a teacher come from God, for no man can perform signs and wonders such as you perform unless God is with him." Jesus gave him this answer: "I solemnly assure you, no one can see the reign of God unless he is begotten from above." *(John 3:1-3)*

As he [Paul] traveled along and was approaching Damascus, a light from the sky suddenly flashed about him. He fell to the ground and at the same time heard a voice saying, "Saul, Saul, why do you persecute me?" "Who are you, sir?" he asked. The voice answered, "I am Jesus, the one you are persecuting. Get up and go into the city, where you will be told what to do." The men who were traveling with him stood there speechless. They had heard the voice but could see no one. Saul got up from the ground unable to see, even though his eyes were open. They had to take him by the hand and lead him into Damascus. For three days he continued blind, during which time he neither ate nor drank. *(Acts 9:3-9)*

NIGHT COUNTRY

ONE ACQUAINTED WITH THE NIGHT,
ONE ACQUAINTED WITH THE NIGHT.

> Off to the hills in prayer — before the dawn arrives.
> Sweating blood in a darkened garden — and the flowers
>   hide.
> Teaching Nicodemus in secret — stars absent from the
>   sky.
> Understanding Peter's tears — the night fire tells all.
> Tortured in body and mind — the sun giving no light.

ONE ACQUAINTED WITH THE NIGHT,
ONE ACQUAINTED WITH THE NIGHT.

> Mary — a dead son nailed to a tree.
> Thomas — filled with blinding doubt.
> John — a master-friend entombed.
> Magdalene — a savior lost too soon.
> Paul — Damascus blinded — zeal crushed.

ONE ACQUAINTED WITH THE NIGHT,
ONE ACQUAINTED WITH THE NIGHT.

> The refugee — without home and family.
> The mentally ill — living daily near the edge.
> The abandoned — cast out and afraid.
> The maligned — name torn away.
> The lost sinner — map and compass stolen.

ONE ACQUAINTED WITH THE NIGHT.
ONE ACQUAINTED WITH THE NIGHT.

One ac - quaint - ed with the night

PRAYER

Gracious and loving God, you too are acquainted with the night. You gave to the world the sun and moon, a greater and lesser light. Yet you entered our darkness and tasted our anguish. Acquaint us now with your light, your Spirit of love. *Amen.*

QUOTATIONS FROM DAG HAMMARSKJOLD

He is one of those who has had the wilderness for a pillow, and called a star his brother. Alone. But loneliness can be a communion.

———

What makes loneliness an anguish
Is not that I have no one to share my burden,
But this:
I have only my own burden to bear.

———

To be able to see, hear and attend to that within us which is there in the darkness and the silence.

———

We can reach the point where it becomes possible for us to recognize and understand Original Sin, that dark counter-center of evil in our nature — that is to say, though it *is* not our nature, it is *of* it — that something within us which rejoices when disaster befalls the very cause we are trying to serve, or misfortune overtakes even those whom we love.[45]

NIGHTMARES

Those who are acquainted with the night are different. There's something about their eyes and voices, the two key instruments of personal revelation, that gives them away. Their eyes contain a depth and glow that comes only with vast experience; their voices come from a different source.

John of the Cross was acquainted with the night. He called these nights the dark night of the senses and of the spirit. Deprivation and nakedness plunged the soul into a void which only God himself could fill. John refused to embrace any created good, no matter how precious, in his striving for union with God. In these nights he traveled alone and the acquaintance turned him into a mystic.

Mary, the mother of Jesus, was acquainted with the night. She stood in the shadow of the cross and watched her son die. Sheer affliction pierced her soul. No consolation would be touched as long as her son suffered. The mysterious bonding of mother and son cannot be captured in words. The horrendous severing of that relationship through a cruel death even more defies expression. All one can say: she was acquainted with the night of affliction and grief.

Is acquaintance with the night necessary for fullness of life? A strange question. Again the mysterious paradox keeps breaking into the human condition: to see well demands darkness; to live one must die; to gain freedom we must surrender all; to save one's life is to lose it. Paradoxes and enigmas work themselves out in the night. No solution is found to the riddle, but a process of living with them is developed. Without the night experience we falter on the way and get lost time and time again.

Deprivation of light can cause nightmares. Acquaintance with the night can be destructive — personal experience can testify to this. Yet there is a graced side to the night and faith harvests in the darkness the presence of the Lord. Stripped of all else we create room in our hearts and lives for the Lord to enter. Were the night not to come, our lives would be too filled with daylight and all its many activities. Acquaintance with the night is a call home to the center of our being.

Longing

MANTRA: **That tears my heart with longing**

SOURCE: Hermann Hesse's "Glorious World"

I feel it again and again, no matter
Whether I am old or young:
A mountain range in the night,
On the balcony a silent woman,
A white street in the moonlight curving gently away
That tears my heart with longing out of my body.

Oh burning world, oh white woman on the balcony,
Baying dog in the valley, train rolling far away,
What liars you were, how bitterly you deceived me,
Yet you turn out to be my sweetest dream and illusion.

Often I tried the frightening way of "reality,"
Where things that count are profession, law, fashion, finance,
But disillusioned and freed I fled away alone
To the other side, the place of dreams and blessed folly.

Sultry wind in the tree at night, dark gypsy woman,
World full of foolish yearning and the poet's breath,
Glorious world I always come back to,
Where your heat lightning beckons me, where your voice calls![46]

PARALLEL REFERENCES

Soon afterward he went to a town called Naim, and his disciples
and a large crowd accompanied him. As he approached the gate of

the town a dead man was being carried out, the only son of a widowed mother. A considerable crowd of townsfolk were with her. The Lord was moved with pity upon seeing her and said to her, "Do not cry." Then he stepped forward and touched the litter; at this, the bearers halted. He said, "Young man, I bid you get up." The dead man sat up and began to speak. Then Jesus gave him back to his mother. *(Luke 7:11-15)*

Hear my prayer, O Lord;
    to my cry give ear; to my weeping be not deaf!
For I am but a wayfarer before you, a pilgrim like all my fathers.
Turn your gaze from me, that I may find respite
    ere I depart and be no more. *(Psalm 39:13-14)*

HEART'S LONGINGS

THAT TEARS MY HEART WITH LONGING,
THAT TEARS MY HEART WITH LONGING.

Jesus' torn heart —
  longing that life conquer the savage sword of death
                                          — Calvary!
  longing that peace touch fragile lives and a weary world
                                          — Pentecost!
  longing that the sweat of blood give meaning to suffering
                                          — Gethsemane!
  longing that blind searchers find healing and salvation
                                          Jericho!
  longing that tombs be empty, hearts filled with joy
                                          — Easter!

THAT TEARS MY HEART WITH LONGING,
THAT TEARS MY HEART WITH LONGING.

Jesus' mercy-filled desires —
  Naim — a mother's tears and the wound of loss.
  Jordan — a cry of repentance and of sin-crushed hearts.
  Cana — the intimacy of love and companionship of wine.
  Galilee — nets mended and the satisfaction of shared
    work.
  Nazareth — home and safe from the madding crowd.

THAT TEARS MY HEART WITH LONGING,
THAT TEARS MY HEART WITH LONGING.

Jesus' deep passions —
  Mary's listening — Bethany — the intimacy of
    understanding
  Peter's profession — Tabor — the glory of faith
  Judas' betrayal — the garden — the hope of fidelity
  Pilate's condemnation — Jerusalem — the cry of justice
  Cleopas' question — Emmaus — the hunger for truth

That tears my heart with long - ing

PRAYER

Jesus, give us entrance into your heart and deepest longings. Teach us that your desires reveal what your kingdom means. Grace us that we might long for what you want even though your will tears our hearts. May we find in your longings a glorious world. *Amen.*

QUOTATIONS FROM HERMANN HESSE

A longing to wander tears my heart when I hear trees rustling in the wind at evening. If one listens to them silently for a long time, this longing reveals its kernel, its meaning.

———

The songs are full of sadness, but the sadness is only a summer cloud, behind it stand trust and the sun.

———

But there is no center in my life; my life hovers between many poles and counterpoles. A longing for home here, a longing for wandering there. A longing for loneliness and cloister here, and an urge for love and community there. I have collected books and paintings and given them away. I have cultivated voluptuousness and vice, and renounced them for asceticism and penance. I have faithfully revered life as substance, and then realized that I could recognize and love life only as function.

———

Prayer is as holy, as sanctifying as song. Prayer is trust, is confirmation. Whoever prays truly does not ask for anything, he merely recounts his condition and his wants, he sings forth his suffering and his thanks, as little children sing.[47]

TRAIN TRACKS

Many hours of my youth were spent walking the train tracks just north of our rural village. Though the sound of summer baseball lured me away, though the shouts of friends called me from the distance, though the benefits of small summer employment offered satisfaction, I clung to the tracks as a spider to his web.

The tracks were empty of trains—at least most of the time. The steel rails pointed north and south to infinity. These iron ribbons told of permanency as well as strength; the decaying wooden ties hinted of mortality and limitation. The silence of the evening walks and the solitude offered by abandoning village and friends gave my heart permission to taste the desires and longings of the human spirit.

Though I was young, deep questions and strange feelings sought entrance into my inexperienced soul: the desire for human and divine touch; the hunger for meaning; the frustration of endless choices, big and small; the mystery of space and time; the confusion of war and hatred; the presence of transcendence and invisible music; the enigma and fear of self.

Torn with unsatisfied longings and unanswered questions, I would hurry back to family and friends. Yet, within the month, even though I suspected the longings would never be satisfied, something would draw me back to the winding ribbon of the railroad tracks. Here was my true home—on the edge of Being. May those tracks always remain in my memory lest I lose my heart and its hungers.

NOTES

1. Jessica Powers, title poem from *The House at Rest* (Pewaukee, WI: Carmelite Monastery, 1984), 9.

2. Graham Greene, *Ways of Escape* (New York: Simon and Schuster, Inc., Pocket Books, 1980), 26, 178, 226, 236, 247.

3. C. S. Lewis, *The Great Divorce* (New York: Macmillan Publishing Co., 1946), 72, 81, 93, 97-98.

4. Flannery O'Connor, *The Habit of Being* (New York: Farrar, Straus and Giroux, Inc., 1979), 354, 452, 476.

5. Meister Eckhart, trans. Raymond Blakney (New York: Harper Torchbooks, Harper & Row Publishers, Inc., 1941), 22, 85, 151, 241.

6. Dante Alighieri, *The Divine Comedy,* trans. Lawrence Grant White (New York: Pantheon Books, Inc., 1948), 10.

7. Goethe, *Faust,* trans. Walter Kaufmann (New York: Doubleday and Co., Inc., 1961), 67.

8. William Shakespeare, *Romeo and Juliet,* III, v, 73-74.

9. C. G. Jung, *Memories, Dreams, and Reflections,* trans. Richard and Clara Winston (New York: Vintage Books, Inc., 1965) 19, 117, 356, 63.

10. *Anne Frank: The Diary of a Young Girl,* trans. B. M. Mooyaart-Doubleday (New York: Doubleday and Co., Inc., 1952), 164, 172, 211.

11. Romano Guardini, *The Lord* (Chicago: Henry Regnery Co., 1954), 22, 125-126, 211.

12. Thomas Merton, *Seeds of Contemplation* (New York: Dell Publishing Co., Inc., 1949), 13, 116, 122, 173.

13. William Styron, *The Confessions of Nat Turner* (Bergenfield, N.J.: New American Library, Inc., 1966), 22, 216, 380.

14. *Story of a Soul: the Autobiography of St. Thérèse of Lisieux,* trans. John Clarke, O.C.D. (Washington, D.C.: ICS Publications, Institute for Carmelite Studies, 1975), 42.

15. William James, *The Varieties of Religious Experience: a Study in Human Nature* (New York: The Modern Library, 1936), 138, 274, 319.

16. *Julian of Norwich: Showings,* trans. Edmund Colledge, O.S.A., and James Walsh, S.J., Classics of Western Spirituality series (New York: Paulist Press, 1978), 196.

17. John Henry Cardinal Newman, *Apologia pro Vita Sua* (Boston: Houghton Mifflin Co., 1956), 209, 244-245.

150

18. Meriol Trevor, *Newman: The Pillar of the Cloud* (New York: Double-day and Co., Inc., 1962), Newman to Mrs. Bowden, 359.

19. Teresa of Avila, *The Interior Castle,* trans. Kieran Kavanaugh, O.C.D., and Otilio Rodriguez, O.C.D., Classics of Western Spirituality series (New York: Paulist Press, 1979), 39-40.

20. Catherine of Siena, *The Dialogue,* trans. and introd. by Suzanne Noffke, O.P., Classics of Western Spirituality series (New York: Paulist Press, 1980), 35, 124, 213, 218.

21. William Shakespeare, *Hamlet,* III, iii, 51-56.

22. *The Cloud of Unknowing and the Book of Privy Counseling,* ed. William Johnston (New York: Image Books, 1973), 58-59.

23. Fyodor Dostoevsky, *The Brothers Karamazov* trans. Constance Garnett (New York: Random House, Inc., 1950), 314, 91, 722, 850-851.

24. Catherine of Genoa, *Purgation and Purgatory: The Spiritual Dialogue,* trans. Serge Hughes, Classics of Western Spirituality series (New York: Paulist Press, 1979), 80.

25. Louis Dupré, *The Deeper Life: An Introduction to Christian Mysticism* (New York: Crossroad Publishing Co., 1981), 73, 62, 40.

26. e. e. cummings, "#91," *100 Selected Poems* (New York: The Grove Press, Inc., 1959), 111.

27. Loren Eiseley, *The Unexpected Universe* (New York: Harcourt Brace Jovanovich, Inc., 1969), 90, 195, 150.

28. Robert Burns, "To a Mouse."

29. Eiseley, *The Unexpected Universe,* 86, 179, 192.

30. Edward Seifert, "Pain," from the series *Spiritual Aids for Those in Renew* (New York: Alba House, 1984), 7.

31. William Shakespeare, *King Lear,* II, iv, 103-106; III, iv, 6-14; III, vi, 102-105.

32. William Shakespeare, *Hamlet,* III, i, 57-83.

33. Ernest Becker, *The Denial of Death* (New York: The Free Press, 1973), 70, 27, 257-258.

34. Percy Bysshe Shelley, "Mutability."

35. Herman Melville, *Moby Dick* (New York: The Modern Library, 1949), 28, 486, 502, 534-535.

36. Robert Browning, "Epilogue to 'Asolando.' "

37. Robert Stone, *A Flag for Sunrise* (New York: Alfred A. Knopf, Inc., 1981), 26, 253, 405.

38. Jessica Powers, "Obscurity," from *The House at Rest,* 43.

39. Matthew Arnold, "Dover Beach."

40. *The Complete Works of St. John of the Cross,* trans. Kieran Kavanaugh, O.C.D., and Otilio Rodriguez, O.C.D. (Washington, D.C.: ICS Publications, Institute for Carmelite Studies, 1973), 421, 447, 629, 77.

41. William Shakespeare, *King Lear,* I, i, 86-93.

42. Thomas Hardy, "The To-Be-Forgotten."

43. Jessica Powers, "The Soul That Cries to God," and "The Cedar Tree," from *The House at Rest,* 21, 62.

44. Robert Frost, "Acquainted with the Night," *The Poetry of Robert Frost,* ed. Edward Connery Latham (New York: Holt, Rinehart and Winston, 1969), 255.

45. Dag Hammarskjold, *Markings,* trans. Leif Sjoberg and W. H. Auden (New York: Alfred A. Knopf, Inc., 1966), 40, 85, 97, 149.

46. Hermann Hesse, "The Glorious World," *Wanderings: Notes and Sketches,* trans. James Wright (New York: Farrar, Straus and Giroux, Inc., 1972), 36.

47. *Ibid.,* 59, 82, 105–106, 74.